ANNA PAVLOVA

ANNA PAVLOVA

V. SVETLOFF

Translated from the Russian by A. GREY

DOVER PUBLICATIONS, INC.

NEW YORK

This Dover edition, first published in 1974, is an unabridged republication of the work originally published in a limited edition by M. de Brunoff, Paris, in 1922. Of the 22 full-color illustrations in the original edition, eight are reproduced in color in this reprint, the rest being shown in black and white.

International Standard Book Number: 0-486-23047-3
Library of Congress Catalog Card Number: 74-75707

Manufactured in the United States of America
Dover Publications, Inc.
180 Varick Street
New York, N.Y. 10014

Вы вступили въ царство
сказокъ и мелодій, какъ новая фея,
ведущая куда-то впередъ... Все отдавъ
имъ полюбилъ. Сама музыка въ
Васъ влюбилась. Теперь вместе съ
Вами, она какъ-бы вновь сверкаетъ
плачетъ, радуется чарусъ, и сво-
бодно несется къ небесамъ...
Благодарилъ Васъ отважная
и безсмертная артистка, за свет-
лую поэзію, за лучскую кра-
соту созданныхъ Вами музыкаль-
ныхъ виденій!

С. Андреевскій

(S. Andreevsky's tribute to Pavlova is given in English on the following page.)

Like to a hitherto unknown fairy, our guide towards new regions, you have entered the realm of legend and melody... And all that remained behind became colourless. Music itself loves you; for, with you, Music glitters, weeps, and rejoices anew : and, enfranchised, soars towards heaven.

We are grateful to you, valiant and immortal artist, for your bright lucid poetry, for the beauty of the musical visions which you call to life.

S. ANDREEVSKY

Pavlova is to dance what a Racine is to poetry, a Poussin to painting, a Gluck to music.

J.-L. VAUDOYER

TABLE OF CONTENTS

LIST OF ILLUSTRATIONS

The wood-cuts are by D. Galanis.
Five head-pieces are reproduced from original engravings by
Canova.
The illustrations in the chapter " Giselle " are reproductions
from wood-cuts by F. Jules Collignon published in
Les Beautés de l'Opéra. *(Paris, Soulié, 1845.)*

FULL-COLOR ILLUSTRATIONS

LÉON BAKST. Water-colour drawing of Pavlova's costume in
" The Sleeping Beauty ". Full page
B. ANISFELD. Water-colour drawing for Pavlova's costume in
" The King's Seven Daughters ". Full page
AIMÉ STEVENS. Portrait of Pavlova. Full page

BLACK-AND-WHITE ILLUSTRATIONS

PREFACE

N my book " Le Ballet Contemporain " (published in 1911) I have attempted to show that however daring and original a new form of art may appear — even if it seems at first to have cropped up suddenly, and irrespective of conditions of time and space — it always has its roots in the past, and remains connected with the art of bygone periods.

The evolution of art, indeed, is governed by the law of succession. The activities of a Fokin, whose influence rescued our ballet from stagnation, seemed at first to constitute a thorough upheaval of the old ballet's traditions. Fokin seemed to do away with all the principles and methods that were Petipa's. He discarded formal symmetry and geometrical arrangements; he interwove the patterns of the movements with those of the sounds, establishing a firm alliance between music and dancing. He was the first to show that it was possible, and indeed necessary, to use extensively, for the purposes of dancing, the symphonic works of the greatest composers, and not the namby-pamby stuff turned out by the appointed ballet-composers. Through him, dancing was united to action, and became the fundamental element of the choregraphic drama; the Ballet grew into one of the chief national forms of art.

Yet all that he has done has its fount in the old ballet of Petipa. Before producing *The Fire Bird* and *Petrushka*, he worked his way, by gradual stages, from the old tradition to the new *(Eunice, Le Pavillon d'Armide)*. And he created " Fokin's style " out of the very same elements that had served to constitute the style of Petipa: viz, out of classical dancing, remodelled in its architecture and proportions so as to become his own.

Suddenly, at the very moment when Fokin's activities were reaching their climax, another innovator appeared : Nijinsky, who started to repudiate all that Fokin had done. In his opinion, Fokin's Ballets were behind the age. They contained in too great a proportion elements of " pure " dancing; they were not altogether free from mawkishness, from a " prettiness " to which Nijinsky took exception. And however strange it may seem, the fact remains that Nijinsky set out to stem the tide of dynamics in dancing, substituting for it the immobility of a bas-relief *(l'Après-midi d'un Faune)*, studies in ethnographical statuary *(le Sacre du Printemps)*, or motions that were, so to speak, synthetic symbols *(Jeux)*. After asserting his conception of the Ballet in the three afore-mentioned works, he proceeded no further.

After him, another reformer sprang up, Miassin, who started to utilise Nijinsky's interpreters in new ventures. He seems to aim at abolishing all that choregraphy has done up to the present day. " Nowadays " he says " while painting, music, and literature have in the course of their evolution passed from romanticism to realism, from realism to impressionism, and thence to cubism, the spirit of dancing remains what it was in the days of romanticism, and has not accomplished the least progress ". Miassin and his votaries allege that Fokin had created a choregraphic style in which " the decadence and artificiality of peace-time asserted themselves to the full"; as to Nijinsky, he was merely " a tenor of the Ballet ".

" But war " they continue " has come to imbue art with virility. There is no longer room for pallid youths adorned with wreaths of pallid roses ". The younger generation of artists places its faith in " muscles of steel ": and Miassin has decided that dancing should progress with the times and conform to their idiosyncrasies. " In his quest for new modes of expression, Miassin has discovered a new range of gestures. Intent on doing away with half-a-dozen obsolete positions of the arms, he has invented a hundred new

Photo Van Riel.

PAVLOVA
IN "LES PRÉLUDES"

ANNA PAVLOVA
PORTRAIT BY SORINE

positions : legs, arms, elbows and head are no longer bound by a complicated, hard-and-fast ritual, but have acquired full freedom and power of expression ".

So keen is Miassin in his repudiation of all that was done in the past, that he rejects even Fokin's theory of a close union between music and dancing. " Until now " he says " people had thought that to each movement a note must correspond. That dancing should come as a counterpoint to music is a fallacy. Dancing is the union of plastics and dynamics. Fokine devoted his care to attitudes that turned choregraphy into a series of *tableaux vivants*, into something like the sets of pictures shown by means of lantern slides. Miassin endows the pictures with life and motion; he magnifies them, he speeds their succession until they follow one another in smooth, continuous sequence. It is no longer a lantern, but a cinematograph ".

In *Parades* Miassin (according to M. Jasmin, a critic from whose article *Une Chorégraphie Nouvelle* I have quoted the above passages) deliberately flings down the gauntlet, and asserts his set purpose to do away with all conventions. In the last lines of the article the writer avers, in obviously hyperbolic terms, that Miassin aroused choregraphic art from stagnation and, by assimilating its tendencies to those of contemporary painting and music, impelled it to accomplish a century's progress at one stroke.

Thus, within half-a-score years, the Russian Ballet underwent several evolutions, or rather revolutions. Never has any theoretical vindication of either Fokin's tendencies or Nijinsky's appeared in any of the interviews granted by them to the Press, or in any of the countless articles written on their work. Fokin especially fought shy of theoretical statements. The genuine artist creates impulsively, under the spell of inspiration; and, as often as not, unconsciously, simply giving vent to the ideas, feelings, visions and fancies of his inner self. He creates because he cannot help so doing, because his instinct is to create, an instinct which in his mind calls for no justification whatsoever — and what are theories but attempts towards justification? As regard Miassin, whichever theories he may have adduced to vindicate his tendencies, the results of his work, viz, the productions for which he is responsible, constitute stronger arguments in his favour or against him that any utterances or disquisitions of his.

What do Miassin's assets consist of? Of a few productions — one cannot call them Ballets — from which dancing as hitherto conceived is practically excluded. His most typical effort, *Parades*, constitutes a caricature of music-hall turns.

In the course of *Parades* a dummy horse appeared on the stage. One dancer was inside the forequarters of the carcass, another inside the hindquarters. As they were unaccustomed to performances of that sort, it occurred that the canvas became distorted in such wise that the dummy resembled a camel rather than a horse. The dancers stamped about frantically whilst the orchestra ceased playing. After that, two music-hall managers, obviously competitors, started to stamp about, each inside his booth, and to quarrel with one another. A female acrobat then did a turn somewhat amateurishly; for a dancer can hardly outrival a professional in the matter of athletics. The episode was not funny, but rather distressing; and for the artist it must have been most annoying.

But, if we are to believe Miassin's apologists, *Parades* is merely a challenge, a protest. Against dancing, against music? One cannot tell, and it does not matter. A production whose purpose is polemical cannot be considered as a work of art : for art and polemics have nothing in common.

Close upon that caricature came several further productions of the grotesque order. *La Boutique Fantasque* lacks originality, being a merely a new edition of *The Imp of the Dolls*, a ballet of the good old times, of a time anterior even to Fokin's reforms. *The Good Humoured Ladies* is the best thing that Miassin has done. Yet, it is merely grotesque, as are *The Three-Cornered Hat* and *Le Chant du Rossignol*. Throughout those productions, the dancers go about frantically stamping their feet — a procedure that in the long run becomes very irksome to the onlooker.

Miassin's work in *The Good-Humoured Ladies*, *Le Rossignol*, and especially *The Three-Cornered Hat*, should not be underrated : his expenditure of energy and his painstaking care deserve recognition, and have not been fruitless, especially as regards the accurate discipline and perfect drilling, down to the minutest details, of the characters and the masses. But in the results of all that formidable labour, there is little that does not leave the spectator cold, or even dissatisfied. All is so cold-blooded, so remorselessly rational, so thoroughly devoid of inspiration and feeling. The whole thing is a " stunt ", carried out upon the stage for a purpose that is purely polemical. There can be no question of creative genius. And that is Miassin's weakest point : his pro-

ductions are governed by the arrogant imperatives of theory —
whereas in true art, theories never herald works, but follow in
their wake.

In his merciless repudiation not only of all that resembles
romance, but even of plain narrative construction, Miassin has
deprived his productions of what ought to remain the Ballet's most
delicate nare : of inspiration, poetic suggestiveness and fancy. He
has transmuted the Ballet into a piece of technical machinery whose
functions are but to bandy rhythms and beats. A momentary flash
— and the whole thing is over. Alas for Fokin, for his dreamlike
Sylphides, his dramatic *Sheherazade,* his tragic *Cleopatra,* his
romantic *Spectre de la Rose,* his sentimental *Carnaval,* his wild
Polovtsian Dances, his fantastic *Fire-Bird,* his wonderfully mystical
Petrushka, and his old-world myths, *Narcisse,* or *Daphnis and
Chloe!* All that output of his is branded as " rubbish ", and grotesque caricatures are brought up to stand in its stead. Certainly,
the grotesque is entitled to a place in the sun — but not to any
monopoly. Caricature is a negative form of creation at best; and,
taken singly, it can hardly be considered as constructive. By repu-
diating all the past, Miassin has gradually done away with all the
movements elaborated during centuries of evolution for the purposes of dancing — and by so doing, with dancing itself. It is
said that he has devised a Ballet without music, which he has not
yet decided to produce.

That stage of evolution once reached, how shall one proceed
further? Either by simply abolishing choregraphy, or, even more
simply, by reverting to the classical Ballet of yore.

If I have dwelt so long upon the doings of the three afore-
mentionned innovators, it was in order to show that the Russian
Ballet has undergone, in fact, convulsions as violent, comparatively
speaking, as those that have shaken Russia's political life to its
foundations. Fokin's revolution was bloodless. Without violence
of any kind, he liberated the Ballet from the obsolete, despotic rules
of academic routine, which in the course of time had become an
absurdity. A free and genuine artist, instinct with live inspiration,
he retained of the old elements all that were live and valuable, using
them to fresh ends in new creations. He worked according to his
untrammelled inspiration and not to a theory.

The brief period of Nijinsky's activities is one of tentative
experiments. Negative tendencies crop up. Elements heralding
Miassin's extremism loom, as yet indistinct, uncertain : the stamping

of feet, the angular, distorted movements, the exaggerations of *Sacre de Printemps*, the slight grotesqueness of *Jeux*.

Last of all came Miassin, with his " Bolshevik " upheaval of choregraphy. He destroyed all the heritage of the past, all that the ages had elaborated and accumulated : and, having laid all waste, he started to edify according to theory. He threw choregraphy into so hopeless a disorder, that the only hope of salvation lay in a return to choregraphy's true function, to classicism.

The question arises, did the Ballet derive some permanent advantage from the experiments that I have recounted, or did it suffer by them? My opinion is that on the whole they did some good. Firstly, because failing those revolutionary excesses, the classical ballet might have remained in it's state of stagnation. And perhaps we should not have witnessed for a long time the wonderful renaissance of classicism to which I have just alluded.

Secondly, I am deeply convinced that of the periods of negation and periods of investigation and discoveries which follow one another, each one leaves behind it some valuable elements, which become incorporated into the very foundations of art. Infatuations and excesses pass by. The chaos and racket of the strife fade away. The heavy artillery of advertisements and polemics is silent. It becomes possible to see things — important or trifling — in their true light. The beautiful but ephemeral blossom dies, the fruit remains, and goes to enrich the assets of art — the art of all times, whose evolution is gradual and slow, and takes place not amidst storm and strife, but during the period of peace favourable to tranquil fruition of the new conquests.

Isadora Duncan's revival of old time dancing; Fokin's romantic conceptions; the elements derived from bas-reliefs and statuary that characterised Nijinsky's productions; even the futurism and cubism of Miassin — all these tributary rivulets help to increase in volume the potent quiet stream that is the classical Ballet. They carry new ideas and new ideals.

Genuine art has never ignored novel ideas. It could not have ignored them : in art, as in all things that are live, stagnation means paralysis and slow death. But with genuine art excesses are incompatible, because the standard of genuine art has always been the sense of proportion. Without that standard, a work will come either as a survival of a style that has become effete and lifeless, or as a childish and extravagant caricature of some kind, daring perhaps, but awkward. Art must work its way from a centre — constituted by all that time has built and taught — to the periphery, *i. e.* to new tendencies, as yet hazy and undetermined. Where to stop on that road from the centre to the periphery is a problem that the genuine artist's intuition and sense of proportion will solve for him. The centre may remain unchangeable : somewhere, near that centre or far from it, is the circumference. The length of the radius is determined by him who prospects — or rather, by the atmosphere of the times in which the prospector is living.

It is no wonder that the Paris of 1920 should have discovered anew the charm and interest of the attitudes, steps and movements belonging to the art of the classical Ballet : five years of excesses of all kind in all the provinces of human activity, art or life, had led to inordinate tiredness.

As regards the Ballet, sudden, kinematographic changes of direction ; movements instinct with frantic agitation ; the disappearance of coherent plots ; the elaborate artificiality of contours, attitudes and formations ; the eagerness with which the new producers sheered off the centre — all that has produced a normal, an unavoidable reaction towards that very centre, *i. e.*, a renaissance of classical dancing.

Pavlova came forth in the fulness of time to satisfy a general craving. She had been away from Paris a long time : she returned with her own troop and repertory, and was hailed with unqualified enthusiasm.

Her reappearance in the *Ville-Lumière*, in that Paris which had always paid a willing and lavish tribute of admiration to Russian art in all its provinces — painting, symphonic music, opera, and especially Ballet — coincided with a season of Serge Diaghilef's Russian Ballet, which during the days of the war had sharply swerved towards extreme cubism ant futurism. Pavlova's Ballet, although open to new forms and new tendencies, remained in accordance with the fundamental traditions of the classical school, and revealed itself as a genuine Academy of Choregraphic Art.

A curious thing was — as one of the Paris critics remarked — that the " National Academy of Music and Dancing " that is, the very conservative Théâtre de l'Opéra, housed Diaghilef's ultra-modernist Ballet, whilst Pavlova and her troop appeared at the more modern Théâtre des Champs-Elysées.

That renaissance of classical dancing came as a revolution to the Paris public, which is never without a modicum of snobbishness in art matters, and — to quote M. Marcel Boulenger's words —

" is prepared to view with favour any attempt to break away from classical tradition; intensely dislikes anything that seems to smack of pedantry or of scholasticism, although to us that very thing may appear fraught with the most precious gifts of the Muses; and chafes under all that originates, if only from the point of view of form, proportion, melody, and tone, in the wonderful, mysterious past. Is there one school of opposition that has endured? At this time of intellectual Bolshevism, of frensy and madness, can those obstinate old classics still hold their own? Yes, they can and they do, precisely as they did in the times of the Renaissance, amid all the vicissitudes and upheavals of the worlds politics ".

Pavlova's reappearance in Paris, at the moment when intellectual Bolshevism and political disorder were at their climax, not only disclosed the possibility of a renaissance, but came as a great relief to all who had kept clear of political turmoil and erratic, freakish, wanton tendencies in art.

A Russian proverb says : " do not pull down the past : it is the foundation of the future ". To define in briefest terms the significance of Pavlova's art, one could find nothing better than that terse proverb, in which the whole wisdom of the nation is epitomised.

THE ORIGIN
OF CLASSICAL DANCING

(Introductory)

I

 LASSICAL dancing originates in the human being's fundamental need for movement. And in the instinct that generates movement, we see the direct result of the human organism's endeavour to give vent to its accumulated vitality. Primitive movements, which resolve themselves into a series of more or less uniform gestures, constitute but the raw material of dancing, and are in themselves quite devoid of aesthetic value. A sequence of movements begins to acquire aesthetic value only when these movements become subordinated to a certain determined order; or, in other words, to rhythm. The sense of rhythm is no less inborn than the need for movement : indeed, the acoustic nerves

and the motory nerves both spring from the *medulla oblonga*. Any excitation affecting the former is transmitted to the latter, with the result that the excitation of both sets of nerves gives birth to one reflex. And the invention of percussion instruments such as Greek crotals, castanets, tambourines, and tom-toms, comes to show the fundamental importance of rhythm in national folk-dancing, even where music is lacking.

Dancing, which corresponds to the human being's need for movement, is likewise the natural expression of his spiritual affections.

It is in dance as well as in song that our first forefathers were wont to express their joys and sorrows, their feelings of exhilaration, of awe, of hate, of love. Like folk-song, dancing obeys the natural laws of number and rhythm, at first crudely perceived, but gradually realised in their fulness, in proportion as civilisation progressed. The order towards which the fundamental principles of that law tend is artistic order, which makes for the organisation of the various elements, numbers and rhythms, tunes or chords, steps or gestures, movements or pauses, into arts-forms.

The evolution of dancing was more gradual, and infinitely slower than that of music. Without harking back to the earlier stages of the progress made by music and dancing respectively, from the Middle Ages to the present day, it will be easily realised that at the time when music had already reached its highest level of organisation and efficiency, acquired the capacity to express in the most various forms the whole range of human aspirations and emotions, dancing was still at a comparatively immature stage of its evolution. It is not until an advanced period of the nineteenth century that it begins to come to its own.

And it is to-day that we actually see for the first time all its potentialities and beauty.

Born at the very moment when humanity appeared, dancing, before becoming an art, underwent a long course of alterations of all kinds. It was associated in turn with astronomy, with magic, with religion, with social or court ceremonies, with allegories and legends.

Before making its appearance on the stage, and acquiring the character of an art-form, its variations and transitional stages were many. But even after it had reached the stage, it had to undergo a long and no less complex evolution before settling down to what we now agree to call the Ballet, or classical dancing.

Phot. d'Ora   Héliog.Schützenberger

ANNA PAVLOVA

PAVLOVA
IN "ORPHÉE"

II

The evolution of classical dancing has alway remained dependent upon two elements: on one hand, the character of the performances in which it was incorporated, and on the other, the changes that periodically cropped up in the matter of stage costumes.

I shall not attempt to draw more than a very summary sketch of the various stages through which dancing, and especially stage dancing, passed before achieving the perfection of the classical Ballet — a history which will be found as attractive as it is instructive, but of which only the principal landmarks need concern us here. Our present object is to ascertain not only what the classical Ballet, as created by our forefathers and fathers, is in itself, and what field it affords to the artists of to-day, but also how far it is rich in potentialities, and as suitable as any other art form to express the aspirations of contemporary souls and to satisfy our eagerness for increasingly perfect and original Beauty.

When it first appeared, the Ballet was a pompous, but comparatively simple and elementary thing.

Court festivities of any kind afforded occasions to produce allegorical Ballets. The first Ballet of that type was staged at Tortona in 1549, on the occasion of the nuptials of the Duke of Milan and Isabel of Aragon. And its success was so great, that forthwith all Italy's potentates, great or small — not excluding the Popes nor the cardinals — started to introduce ballets among the entertainments given at their courts. The productions were of a mixed kind, comprising allegorical *tableaux vivants*, music and recitation.

During the reign of Louis the Fourteenth, pantomime took the place of recitation; and the Ballet, borrowing its subjects from the Greek and Roman mythologies, departed gradually from its original character of a *divertissement*: it started to discard the motley conventionalities inherent to its primitive form, and to acquire the dramatic qualities of the real stage-play.

Louis the Fourteenth also decided that his troop of dancers should perform at the Royal Academy of Music for the general public. And in 1662, he founded the first Academy of dancing.

Although the Ballet was thenceforth provided with a " plot ", it did not acquire its independence forthwith: it was merely transmuted from a *Ballet-Divertissement* into a *Ballet-Opéra* — a type in which the dances provided for the entertainment of the audience remained altogether unconnected with the operatic plot. It followed an invariable and stereotyped course : *Passepieds* were danced in the prologue, *Musettes* in the first act, *Tambourins* in the second; the following acts comprised both *Chaconnes* and *Passepieds*. The subjects of those productions were always borrowed from the old mythologies. In 1683 Lully, who was the manager of the Paris Opera founded by the Royal Academy of Music, gave for the first time permission to female dancers to appear in the Ballet. Their first appearance — a momentous event indeed, and fraught with important consequences — took place in a work named *le Triomphe de l'Amour*. Up to Lully's time, all female parts had been impersonated by men wearing masks. Lully's reform introduced a greater variety in attitudes, movements and dancing, besides doing away with the absurd practice of masks.

Thus the Ballet became endowed with greater beauty and more genuine vitality. But even under these new conditions the Opéra-Ballet, until the second half of the eighteenth century, remained entirely conventional, and moderately satisfactory from the point of view of scenic adequacy. It was still pratically devoid of pantomimic action, that is, of the element which now constitutes the dramatic part of the Ballet.

Under those circumstances, what were the performers to do? Failing the possibility to express human affections and passions, they found themselves restricted to pure dancing. And that art the choregraphic schools and the leading dancers started to promote and cultivate without any ulterior object. From that time on, classical dancing holds the field alone, and progresses rapidly.

III

The changes that took place in the dancers' costumes also played an all important part in the evolution of classical technique. And the whole history of the Ballet is closely bound with the history of dancing costumes.

The transition from the heavy, ample, clumsy dresses worn by the dancers of the time of Louis the Fourteenth to the light, flimsy tunics in use in the nineteenth century was long and laborious.

As already mentioned, no woman had appeared in a Ballet before 1662. The ladies of the Court supported Lully's bold innovation, and many of them even took part in the Ballets. For instance, the members of the first *corps de ballet* were the Princesse de Conti, Mademoiselle de Nantes, and other of high rank. But they wore their inconvenients court toilettes, which seriously interfered with their freedom of movement and comfort, and caused them to appear more like slowly moving puppets than living human beings.

The famous dancer Noverre informs us that professional dancers did not spring up until much later. And they in turn wore heavy court dresses, most unsuitable for the performance of mythological ballets.

What could the dances be so long as that heavy armour interfered not only with free breathing, but with the very freedom of the movements, concealing the lines of the figure and rendering that figure heavy and rigid? Obviously, they had to be slow, and to consist of cautious motions, maintained throughout in the horizontal plane, to the tunes of a music that remained more or less uniform, and was interspersed with long pauses for curtsies and obeisances which came to provide now and then a much needed rest for the fatigued performers. Those dances were altogether in keeping with the atmosphere of stateliness, splendour, and stiffness that prevailed at Court.

In 1721, viz, about forty years later, the famous Camargo made her appearance. The skirts she wore were shorter by a few inches, leaving the ankles uncovered. So bold a disregard for tradition was considered scandalous, and society expressed its disapproval most emphatically.

Slight as it was, this reform in the costume enabled Camargo to break out of the stronghold of the minuets and pavanes, and to experiment in novel movements and steps of the classical order. And naturally enough, the example set by her was followed by other dancers. The disturbance created by the innovation gradually subsided; and after a time all fell in with the new order or things. A famous picture by Lancret, and the *Variation du temps de la Camargo,* which is part of the ballet *Ruses d'amour* produced at the Marinsky Theatre, enable us to judge to what extent the artist's costume was, as alleged, " immodest ", and her dancing " daring ".

The dancers of the time of Louis the Fifteenth, whether they impersonated the ladies of a court, the Bacchants of Greek mythology, or the nymphs of the woods, continued to wear heavy court dresses thus slightly shortened. This attire had become, so to speak, a traditional uniform, quite devoid of connexion with the parts played. Naturally the dancing remained unaltered in style, slow, and restricted to the horizontal plane.

The first appearance of the light Greek tunic took place in London, on the stage of the Theatre Royal, Covent-Garden. It was Mademoiselle Sallé, impersonating Galathea in the ballet *Pygmalion*, who made the bold venture. She came off with flying colours.

In 1761 a new star arose : Mademoiselle Guimard — a dancer who, we are told, " *avait des prétentions à la comédie* ". She endeavoured to introduce dramatic expression in her dancing.

With the close of the French Revolution, the problem of dress came very much to the front. The Revolutionists borrowed their ideals from Republics of old times, and ascribed no small importance to externals. The reformation of costume was laid great stress upon. Even in Russia, Peter the Great decreed that *Kaftans* should be worn shorter, and beards shaven off. External apparances, obviously, come to express the cast of the mind. During the French Revolution and the Directoire, the female raiment was a close imitation of the old Greek tunic. After 1793, the fashion of flimsily veiled nakedness set in. The old garb carried with it old prejudices, and those prejudices were being set aside. In his book " *la Danse* ", M. Roul Charbonnel writes :

" The *Merveilleuses* reduced this costume to a mere veil, which revealed more than it concealed. Sleeves and skirts were suppressed, all non-transparent materials discarded. The dresses were made of thin gauzes and thinner crêpes. A contemporary author writes : " The nakedness of the Greeks and Romans, the draperies appearing in statuary, serve as models for female apparel. The women go about bare-legged, and in Greek dress — or rather undress. One step further, and they would be stark naked. " And on the boundary of the two worlds — the Revolution drawing to its close and the Empire gradually setting in — careless France was dancing... "

Thus did the admiration for bygone times establish the reign of the Greek tunic. On the stage, that tunic was worn shorter, disclosing the legs of the dancers. But for the sake of social conventions, it soon became necessary to avoid actual nakedness. To that effect, Maillot, the costumier of the Paris Opera, invented the knitted, flesh-coloured tights that were named after him *maillots*. (Certain historians, however, are of opinion that the *maillot* was invented at an earlier date). Those tights solved the problem to the satisfaction of all. Even the Pope permitted their use on the stage of the theatres under his jurisdiction — though with the restriction that they were to be of a deep blue colour, so as not to resemble the bare flesh. Anyhow, the human figure had come to its own.

Tights rendered the shortening of the tunic possible. By successive stages, that tunic converted itself into the dancing costume of our times, which became the stereotyped garb of the classical ballet-dancer, as conventional as the cumbersome court attire had been in its own time. For, whereas of yore all the goddesses of Olymp had appeared in court dresses, thenceforth all Ballet characters, whether Greek goddesses or modern peasant girls, appeared and danced in gauze tunics. The costume had changed, but the principle was the same, and artistic fitness remained ignored.

Those gauze tunics were still fairly long, reaching half way between the knee and the ankle (1830-1840). But in proportion as the technique of classical dancing progressed, the skirts became shorter. A number of Italian dancers, specially proficient in the complexities of technique, wore them as short as was possible; and the dancers of the times of Pucchi — the seventies — were in shape not unlike spinning-tops.

Michael Fokin was the first to take up the cudgels against that shape of tunic, and against tunics of all shapes so far as they were not in keeping, ethnologically and chronologically, with the style of the Ballets produced.

IV

The better to describe the evolution of dancing, it was necessary to give the above short summary of the variations in the apparel worn by dancers on the stage — variations with which that evolution remains so closely connected.

The dignified, slow and quiet movements of the Minuet, the Pavane, or the Gavotte, are fully explained by the weight and length of the court dress with its paniers. One could hardly imagine a dancer in that attire performing a classical variation of the type now in favour.

As soon as the shortening of the skirts gave freedom to the limbs, it became possible, and even necessary, to resort to lighter and nimbler movements. The dancers were no longer confined to the horizontal plane, but began to acquire command of the vertical plane. The tendency toward high leaps started to counteract the immutable laws of gravity, and dancing acquired a more buoyant, ethereal character. In proportion as the costume grows shorter, that new character asserts itself more definitely.

Thus choreography, with the evolution of costume, undergoes fundamental alterations. One may say that the birth of classical dancing coincided with the appearance of the tunic. As soon as dancers acquired freedom of movements, they started to invent new steps, progressing from the primary elements of classical choregraphy towards its complete syntax.

We know that Camargo practised the *entrechat*, of which she use to perform five or seven in succession, winding up by striking an attitude. But in fact, of all the standard achievements in the matter of modern classical choregraphy, the *entrechat* alone did not come into use before the dancer's attire had been further altered; it came to perfection in 1750 or thereabouts, when Mademoiselle Lamy used to execute six or eight in succession without any apparent effort. From 1766 to 1800, *entrechats* were so much the fashion, in the ballroom as well as on the stage, that complaints began to be made about the abuse of that very effective step. The *entrechats* were executed in even sets *(entrechats deux, quatre, six, huit)* or in odd *(entrechats trois, cinq, sept)*.

Mademoiselle Heinel, a dancer of the Stutgardt Theatre, invented another step, no less effective, the *pirouette*, which was to be used without measure during the period of Italian classical ballets. Mademoiselle Heinel appeared on the stage of the Paris Opera in 1766, together with Mademoiselle Ferville, and delighted the audience with the novelty of her pirouettes.

Gardel and Vestris improved upon that step and invented another, which in turn was incorporated into classical choregraphy; the *rond de jambe*. And, following in Mademoiselle Heinel's wake, they invented what is called *la grande pirouette à la seconde*.

Of late, the art of the *pirouette* progressed further, and dancers learnt to perform two or three *pirouettes* in succession. The *grande pirouette*, ending in an attitude or an arabesque, corresponds to the pause in the music.

It is said that Madame de Maintenon invented the *sisonne*, a step that enjoyed the greatest vogue during the first years of the eighteenth

ANNA PAVLOVA ET H. STOWITTS
dans « La Péri »

century. Of late, it has merged into the *assemblé*. Gradually, all the elements of classical choregraphy made their appearance; the *cabrioles*, simple, double, or lateral; the *jetés*, the *grands jetés*, the *jetés développés* or *battus;* the *jetés en tournant*, the *échappés*, the *fouettés*, and all others.

V

To describe the origin and progress of each of these steps would be a long task, and one that does not properly come within the scope of the present work. My only purpose in referring to the matter was to show that under the influence of two factors — one, the lack of dramatic elements in the Ballets of the eighteenth century; the other, the periodical reforms of the dancers' garb — classical dancing developed to a prodigious extent. Stage dancing, having once entered the path of virtuosity, extended the technique of choregraphy to its utmost limits.

As soon as the shortening of the tunic gave free scope to virtuosity, two schools in Europe resolutely devoted themselves to developing technique. But while the French school continued to adhere to the quiet, measured style of the Minuet, in Italy (where the ground had been prepared by lively folk-dances, such as the Tarantella) choregraphy rapidly assumed a style founded upon the display of nimbleness, and at times verging upon the grotesque.

A whole series of Italian dancers, who were very much in vogue during the 'eighties, introduced elaborate virtuosity upon the Russian stage. And the Russian dancers started to out-rival them. Ballet-masters followed suit, and encouraged all excesses in technique, devoting all their care to promoting virtuosity of the feet and legs. The result was that no attention was given to the proper action of the torso and arms. The harmonious cooperation of the several parts of the human body was lost sight of. And in dancing, the attitudes and movements of the head, shoulders, torso, and arms, are as important as those of the legs. An artistically minded connoisseur can hardly enjoy even the most skilful *jetés en tournant* executed by a dancer who pays no proper attention to the posture of her head, shoulders, and torso, and holds her arms ungracefully. For then the result is, not artistic dancing, but a mere *tour de force*, whose proper place is in the ring of a circus. The same may be said of the famous *fouettés*. The fashion for them was started in Russia by the most skilful of Italian "technician" dancers, Pierina Leniani. The Russian dancers copied her eagerly. And among the audiences, the custom began to prevail to count aloud the number of the *fouettés* executed in succession by a dancer. But in such displays there was no beauty whatever.

The famous Noverre has said, in his *Lettres sur les Arts imitateurs en général et sur la Danse en particulier*, that " if thirty dancers are performing pirouettes in sets of six each, the chances are that in the course of a couple of hours, they will have accomplished between them over a thousand gyrations. But the dancing dervishes gyrate with far greater speed, and accomplish a far greater number of pirouettes. Yet who would dream of calling them artists?"

Genuine art is a matter of soul, not of technique only. Without soul there can be no art, but only an empty form. Even in those faraway times, Noverre had realised that a dancer could never be an artist unless she possessed both mastery of technique and the capacity to express the emotions of the soul.

It is but rarely that those two orders are found in one artist. For dancers, men or women, devote themselves to training their limbs without bestowing a thought upon the education of their minds. They scorn to study the language of the emotions. And yet, dancing devoid of inner meaning is but an empty display of virtuosity. If a Balletmaster's production consists not of expressive attitudes and movements translating the play of emotions, but merely of brilliant steps and meaningless pirouettes; if it constitutes, not an interesting poem, but a trumpery spectacle of soulless dancing, then there can be no question of genuine art.

Thus did Noverre, the father of the modern Ballet, express himself by word and deed. But his precepts sunk into oblivion.

Towards the end end of the nineteenth century, the technique of Ballet-dancing, as practised by the Italian school, became so excessive, so complicated in its quest for virtuosity, that classical dancing found itself in a blind alley, and on the verge of losing all its artistic significance, to become a species of meretricious acrobacy. For some time it remained at a standstill.

An art that stagnates ceases to be an art. The senseless repetition of mechanical movements, however skilful those movements, becomes pure routine, devoid of artistic interest. And thus did the classical Ballet decay upon the best choregraphic stages of Europe.

It dies out year by year, in the rut of empty virtuosity, far from all that was art. The last few years of the nineteenth century showed the Ballet at its very worst.

All those misuses and abuses of technique, to the detriment of all other elements of the choregraphie art, brought the Ballet down to the level of mere acrobatic shows, and suscitated a necessary reaction. All were sick of classical dancing, and had ceased to take any interest in the nimble *pirouettes*, the brillant *entrechats*, the clever capers; and even the once famous *fouettés* would be greeted with a perplexed smile.

VI

But classical dancing, the very foundation of choregraphic art, could not be allowed to die out in the country where the cult of art constitutes one of the main elements of the national spirit.

Classicism flourished in Russia during the whole of Petipa's period. The dancers' education was conducted according to severely classical principles. And but for Petipa's strenuous and persistent activities in that direction, Russia would not possess to-day her wealth of well-trained, expert dancers of all description. The tradition of the " school " was handed oven from generation to generation, and remains live to the present day. Fokin inherited from Petipa a priceless treasure. And what he in turn accomplished has shown that the plastic art bequeathed to us by ancient Greece, far from being threatened with death, still has a bright future.

Petipa stands out with unsurpassed distinction among all the choregraphists of the nineteenth century, and his name will forever remain prominent in the history of the Russian Ballet.

After him appeared other Ballet-masters, some continuing and developing his tradition, others tampering with it and doing their best to ruin it. But there was no question of new *versus* old. Those two terms, when all is said and done, have but a relative value. What is old at one time was new at some other : what is new will in time become old. Talent, however, is endowed with everlasting youth. And one may say the same of the essential elements of art, of those elements that in the hands of talent go to the creation of beautiful works. For all those reasons, classical dancing is imperishable.

The psychological foundations of artistic creation remain to the present time imperfectly ascertained. It is doubtful whether any satisfactory reply could be found to the question why one human being will select as his medium prose, another proetry, a third music, a fourth painting, a fifth sculpture, a sixth the poetry of attitudes and gestures — that is choregraphy. Some principle, hidden in the very depths of the artist's soul, gives his creative temperament its psychological foundation and sets its course. One thing, however, is certain : that in the soul of the choregraphic artist lives an element of " rhythmical self-determination ", which impels him to exercise his creative instinct in the provinces of form and rhythm.

According to Mr. Kniazef, the author of an interesting book entitled " Principles of aesthetics relating to the art of the Ballet ", the actor himself is the main element of scenic art : the principle of that art consists essentially in the rhythmic movements of the body : that is, in the correspondence between his inner organic rhythms and the rhythms he gives to his impersonation. There is a great analogy between the spoken drama and wordless choregraphy : words, in a dramatic performance, are simply movements transmuted into sounds. The Ballet, considered as a choregraphic drama, is founded upon the rhythms of movements and their mutual affinities. Therefore, in the Ballet, the organic principle of movement, governed by the principle of rhythmical self-determination, gives birth to dancing : that is, graceful movements informed with emotional expression as well as with plastic beauty.

An artistically conceived and skilfully executed Variation or Adagio is as valuable, and fulfils its aesthetic purpose as well, as a lyrical or elegiac poem. Dancing, as well as verse, may teem with poetic expression, imagination, harmony, may be rich in rhythms and faultless in form.

Of course, each form of art has its own range of expression; and the forms of emotions which it expresses best may be different from those to whose expression the other arts are suited. It may be difficult to convey in words the emotions which make the beauty of a piece of music, of a picture, of a dance. That is because words are so far from music and dance and painting. Poetry, by virtue of its rhythms and cadences, comes far nearer to music than either painting or prose. In dancing there is a magic virtue which partakes of the magic of all other arts : of music, of poetry, and to a degree of painting. For dancing is design as well as rhythm. And as we shall see, whereas words often fail as interpreters of the beauty of dancing,

dancing can do full justice (and more than justice) to the beauties of words.

Rhythm is the guiding principle of life throughout the universe. The poet, in the throes of creation, expresses the rhythms of his inspiration in verse; the musician, in melody; the choregraphic artist, in dance. Rhythm asserts itself in painting, in sculpture, in architecture — its character then being static, not dynamic. In Russia, art criticics have always called for "ideas" in works of art, with the result that many artists of merit have been led astray by a misguided quest for "ideas". In course of time, the art of the Ballet came to be branded by the critics as of small account, because it remained devoid of ideas. I myself have met critics who, in order to demonstrate how meaningless the Ballet was, were wont to repeat threadbare conundrums such as : " How can dancing make clear to the onlooker, for instance, that vegetables have become dearer in consequence of a protracted drought?" And I hardly dared explain to such people that it would be likewise impossible to find in the extraction of the square root a fit topic for lyrical poetry, or to give out in music the penal laws applicable to offences coming under the jurisdiction of the police-courts.

However strange the fact, there remain nowadays people who cannot realise that each art creates within its own province only; that the rhythmic element in dancing, which has an aesthetic value of its own, can and must assert itself freely and fully without the intervention of the slightest element of purely rational meaning.

All the aesthetic significance of classical dancing resides in the apparent enfranchisement of the human body from the laws of gravity.

The centre of gravity constitutes for Ballet-dancing a condition *sine qua non*. A dancer's centre of gravity is situated in the lumbar region, at the point where the spine ends. No attitude, no movement or step should, whether the body is supported on one foot or on both. displace that centre. G. Desrat, in his *Dictionnaire de la Danse*, writes : " The weight of a dancer standing on one foot is divided into two parts which are equal to half the weight of the whole mass. The slightest movement causes the central line of gravity to follow the axis of the leg that supports the body ". And it is in this balance, unaltered by movements of any kind, that consists the particular form of grace which finds its full artistic expression in dancing. Dancing, as a plastic art, utilises the properties of form and the mutual relati onship of forms in space, exactly as music utilises sonorous form and their mutual relationship in time. But dancing, comprising in itself, besides plastic elements, a rhythmic principle, possesses a significance deeper than that of arts which avail themselves of one element of expression only.

In the depths of the human mind and soul, there are many moods and fancies that can find their proper expression neither in poetic discourse, nor in painting, nor in statuary : subconscious impressions, vague dreams, impulsive gloom or joy, outbursts of emotions, all those elements come within the province of what the Russian poet Fet describes as " poetry deprived of its wings, poetry that remains imprisoned in the heart as a bird in a cage ". And it is in those obscure subconscious regions of the human soul, striving to associate with the rhythm of the universe, that the fundamental elements of plastic lyriscism, whose creative processes are closely connected with those of music, lie.

That is the reason why it would be no less absurd to ask, as the uninitiated often do, what a certain Variation represents, or what a certain Adagio is meant to convey, than it would be to look for the precise meaning of each of Chopin's Nocturnes or Preludes. They are the expression of moods, but not a verbal expression, nor one that can be made the subject of a cut-and-dried analysis. It is a song that must speak to the feelings; whoever is incapable of responding to that song is incapable of appreciating it.

After having thus attempted to describe the origin of classical dancing and its importance in the art of choregraphy, it remains to devote a few words to the infinite variety and complexity of the steps that classical dancing comprises.

In proportion as the art of dancing progressed further, it came to stand in need of new technical resources, in order to give full expression to the plastic symphony in space which constitutes its object. The increase in the number of steps enables the dancers to achieve more complex combinations of elements, rhythms, and colours.

The classical steps, emanating from one another, or contrasting with one another, or coming as a complement of one another, constitute so to speak the alphabet in which choregraphy expresses its purport. Organised into a system, they embody the lexicography, etymology and syntax of choregraphic art : that is, in other terms, its complete grammar. And it is only after having learnt the idiom of dancing to the full that one can express oneself in its prose or in its poetry. However gifted a man may be, he will prove unable adequately to create so long as he has not mastered the technique of his art. A dancer who lacks schooling — that is, who has not systematically assimilated the technicalities of dancing, who lacks proficiency — will always rank among the mere amateurs, not among those capable of genuine creative work. She will never be able to express her conceptions fully and freely before she has mastered the idiom of her art. For that reason, the school of classical dancing, the academical school, constitutes the very foundation of choregraphy.

VII

The above definition of classical dancing does not imply that it is debarred from progress. But its progress does not consist in the destruction of its inherited wealth. What time, labour, and genius have built, cannot be suppressed by a few revolutionary innovators, whose dream is to make a fresh start after a clean sweep, and to erect a new and magnificent structure out of nothing. No one man, however great his gifts, is capable of creating the necessary materials, which in the natural course of things are the outcome of centuries of labour. A madman only would conceive the notion of ravaging the splendid edifice of classical choregraphy in his morbid thirst for innovation or hatred of tradition. Evolution spells betterment, but not revolution. The evolution of classical dancing can and must be governed by the following principles :

1° It is necessary to do away with all that has become definitely antiquated and meaningless. Technical tricks, when they have sunk to the level of mere acrobacy, cease to be interesting. The nonsensical and inartistic *fouettés* are a case in point, and their disappearance would be no loss to choregraphy.

2° New technical resources should be invented and made available. In that matter, the range open to a dancer of talent is wide. Pavlova, — whose technique will be described in a further chapter of this book devoted to her choregraphical genius — has enriched the art of classical dancing with a number of innovations remarkable for their artistic significance and beauty. Those creations of hers will take a permanent place among the choicest of classical steps, side by side with Camargo's *entrechats* and Heinel's *pirouettes*.

3° The boundless resources of classical choregraphy should be adjusted to the spirit and requirements of the times. The choregraphists of yore paid no attention to the quality of the music with which their productions went. Those of to-day rightly hold that there should be an organic link between the music and the dancing. The symphony of movements and the symphony of sounds should merge into one another. In the olden time, the dances of a Ballet were considered merely as *divertissements*, unconnected with its subject and action. Now the Ballet is a choregraphic drama, and fulfils Noverre's conception — a conception which he did not carry beyond theory — of a dramatic plot intelligibly carried out. Modern choregraphists no longer treat dances as mere *divertissements,* but have given the Ballet its proper function, that of a logical outcome of the plot, a fundamental element of the action. Likewise the expressive possibilities of pantomime, previously overlooked, have now come to their own, and cooperate with plastic expression. That cooperation has created " dramatised dancing ", the supreme exponent of which is Pavlova.

4° The few valuable innovations that are the residue of all the experiments made by the various innovators previously referred to should be incorporated into the classical Ballet.

Thus will choregraphic classicism follow a sound and normal course of evolution, remaining the foundation of the art of the Ballet and the source of all improvements and innovations.

FIRST
PART

PAVLOVA

AS A

CLASSICAL DANCER

I

ET it be said that no organisation has ever supplied the stage with so great a number of classical dancers, nor with dancers so dissimilar in styles and in talent, as the Imperial Russian Ballet.

Russia has produced standard companies of classical dancers, proficient in the science of choregraphy, and from their earliest childhood onward initiated into the best principles and traditions of their art. And if choregraphy has flourished so wonderfully in that country, it is owing to an unusually favourable concourse of artistic conditions. The theatres of Moscow and Petrograd possessed their own model schools of dancing. Ballet-masters such as Petipa, teachers such as Eugénie Sokolova, Gherdt, Cecchetti, and Gerthen superintended the tuition, and the public evinced a keen interest in all that pertained to the art of dancing; so that ballet performances were an everyday occurrence.

It is to the Russian corps-de-ballet, that truly peerless body, and to the artists responsible for its training, that we owe the supreme masterpieces of dancing. And it is from its ranks that have sprung up solo dancers of outstanding merit, dancers who have made ballet-dancing famous.

Almost all the Russian *ballerine* have gone through their term in the corps-de-ballet. And many of them might well have made a successful appearance on the chief stages of Europe, where towards the end of the nineteenth century, the ballet, alas, was steadily declining.

No single theatre has ever mustered so great a number of choregraphic stars as that of Petrograd or that of Moscow. Among the glories of these two stages are Pavlova, Kszessinska, Preobrajenska, Trefilova, Karsavina, Egorova, Roslavleva, Kyasht, Gheltzer, Karalli; and many others, less outstanding, yet of sterling excellence, might be mentioned.

While remaining faithful to the principles of the classical school, those artists have created a considerable variety of choregraphic styles; and each of them has developed her own, according to her idosyncrasies, her individual tastes, her particular conception of rhythm.

There can be, it should seem, no common measure between the sheer technique of a Kszessinska and the elegant methods of a Preobrajenska. Yet, despite all dissimilarities, both artists bear the stamp of the same school, discernible in the perfection of their virtuosity. Both are endowed with a remarkable capacity for expression; but they do not achieve expression in the same way. Both are excellent mimes, but in different ranges : that of Kszessinska being the drama, and that of Preobrajenska, comedy. Yet again, Trefilova is no mime, but dancer first and last. Her classical dances are so many wonderful instances of finish. Each one reveals itself as an indiscerptible whole and a source of rare delight for the beholder. Both Karsavina and Kyasht are original dancers; but their respective styles have hardly anything in common. As " intent in dreaminess " as is Pushkin's Tatiana, Karsavina is the very antithesis of Kyasht, who resembles Olga in Eugen Onieghin, " always merry and with never a care ".

Karsavina, before deciding in favour of the lyric drama, devoted much time to testing her own individuality. Catholic in her artistic tastes, endowed with a strong personality, keenly interested in new forms of art, she swayed from the strictest classicism to the boldest modernism. Kyasht, on the contrary, forthwith selected, among the classical forms, those most imbued with light grace and coquetry, and adopted their style as her own. Never has she given a thought to ambitious schemes, never has she yielded to the lure of " ideas " : but in her own dancing, thoroughly devoid of any particular tenour or drift, she maintains a very high level of charm and attractiveness. Egorova, especially during the last few years of her career on the stage of the Imperial theatres, has asserted herself as a dancer of the academic School. Her dancing, perhaps somewhat cold, but noble and aristocratic in character, included none of the meretricious excesses to which too many artists resort in order to curry favour with their audiences. Roslavleva was a most promising dancer, whose career was cut short by an untimely death. Gheltzer's technique was that of a true classical Ballerine, who in the more impassioned kinds of dances was at times somewhat brusque and abrupt. Karalli, on the contrary, was remarkable for the sweetness and gentleness of her style and expression.

II

In that wonderful garden, teeming with the rarest and most precious flowers that expert choregraphic culture had ever brought to bloom, Pavlova appeared, and at once shone forth in surpassing grandeur and originality. The best judges realised all of a sudden, by intuition rather than by a train of reasoning, that here was an artist endowed with prodigious talent and an individuality which contained in itself, as does a crystal prism, all the colours and manifold shades of the solar spectrum. Even at the moment when she first appeared on the stage, it was possible to hail her as a diamond of the purest water, which lacked nothing but the final touches of the polishing-wheel. The course of time, and the artist's conscientious and intelligent labour have supplied those touches, and the beautiful gem now stands perfect before our eyes, lustrous and splendent with all the iridescent lights of the rainbow.

While every one of the dancers mentioned in the foregoing

Photo S. Bransburg.

PAVLOVA PRACTISING

Photo S. Bransburg.

PAVLOVA PRACTISING

pages was developing her own particular gifts and specialising in the line that best suited her individuality, Pavlova continuously revealed some new aspect of her versatile artistic temperament. At first, she delighted her audiences by the buoyancy and lightness of her dancing. One had never seen such " ballons " nor such leaps. She was like a breeze, a flash, something transparent and elusive, a vision from some wonderful fairy tale. Her far-reaching " envols" seemed to carry her away from the earth, in defiance of the laws of gravity. That extraordinary lightness forthwith set her apart from all the dancers in whose company she came to appear. It was an idiosyncrasy, a gift that was hers alone. The others, however great their skill and merits, remained in comparison *terre à terre.*

It is curious fact that most of the dancers whose virtuosity is essentially technical, such as Leniani, Kshessinska, Preobrajenska, Trefilova, are of a square build. Pavlova, on the contrary, is slim and frail. Her arms being comparatively long, her gestures are ample, easy, plastic, and shapely, in perfect coordination with the movements of the remainder of her body. Her hands possess a life of their own, an independent power of expression. Her feet, wonderfully shaped, are remarkable for the slenderness and power of the ankle and the high arch of the instep; and this peculiarity endows her " pointes " with unusual beauty. When she is standing on tiptoe, the sole of her foot is absolutely vertical, instead of forming with the floor an angle of forty-five degrees — as is often the case with dancers whose instep is not adequately trained. The smallness of her bones, her utter freedom from superfluous flesh, and the elasticity of her muscles, render her body marvelously supple and plastic.

Her ethereal volatility conquered her forthwith a place of honour among the galaxy of choregraphic talents around her.

It is, I think, that organic specificness of her gifts as a dancer, that imponderability and aerial buoyancy of hers, that have carried her for good and all into the enchanted realm of Romanticism. And Romanticism has withheld from her none of its secrets. She became a princess in the remote kingdom of Dreams, Phantasms, Sylphs, Dryads, Naiads and Fairies ; a princess born of magic dreams, of elegy and romance, of those ballads that express a whole epoch and have created a romantic style of their own.

She has been called the modern Taglioni. We do not know anything positive about Taglioni's dancing. In her days, dancing was not described, except perhaps for some short description of purely theoretical character.

We may however derive a fairly accurate notion of her art from the writings of contemporary authors who were interested in the Ballet, such as Théophile Gautier, Jules Janin, Philarète Chasles, and a few others. What those authors say seems to point out that her dancing, generally speaking, resembled Pavlova's in style. But Taglioni was not beautiful. And assuredly her technique must have been inferior to the technique of to-day.

I have said that from the very outset of her career, Pavlova was signalised for her aerial grace and lightness. At that time, she had not yet acquired her technical proficiency. And never did she display an interest in the type of Ballet that is entirely founded on the display of purposeless virtuosity.

After her first appearence as *Giselle,* the dramatic gifts with which she was so richly endowed revealed themselves in their plenitude. They were so great, so prodigious, that none could see her without being stricken with wonder. The spectators followed with breathless interest her acting in the first act, and especially her wonderful rendering of the two tremendously difficult scenes — her loss of reason and her death — in which she brought to bear an incredible power of expression. Her appearance in that part constitutes a red-letter day in the chronicles of the Russian Ballet.

Pavlova had been compared with Virginia Pucchi — which is no less fallacious than to compare her with Taglioni. Pucchi's dramatic temperament was entirely different in character from Taglioni's. In all she did she would remain close to actual life, and her Italian temperament imparted a striking realism to her impersonations. In all essentials, her style of pantomimic expression remained similar to the style of choregraphic expression adopted by the Italian school. Whereas Pavlova has made of *Giselle* a drama that, whilst remaining graphic and live, is beautified by profundity and keenness in its conception and carrying out; a wonderful tragedy of feminine sweetness, pain, and despair. And this she accomplished by means entirely different from those to which Pucchi used to resort. If a comparison were at all wanted, one might say that Pavlova's dramatic talent is most closely related with that of Eleonora Duse. In the impersonations of both, we admire the same poetry of feminine grace and soulful passion, the same simplicity of means, the same supreme force of expression — due perhaps to that very simplicity.

The part of *Giselle* was created by Carlotta Grisi, to whose rendering of it Théophile Gautier, the author of that ballet, has himself born testimony. After Grisi, no dancer proved capable of playing the part successfully. Alone Pavlova accomplished its resurrection, and thereby the resurrection on the Russian stage of the whole period of Romanticism.

Giselle had brought to light both aspects of Pavlova's talent : her dramatic gifts and her aerial buoyancy. But when Pavlova appeared at Paris in 1920, she revealed a new gift which came as a surprise to all who had not seen her for a long time : a wonderful command of classical technique.

The admirers of Leniani, Kshessinska, Trefilova, and other great exponents of technique, could never had dreamed that it was possible to make further progress in that province. It seemed natural to suppose that the utmost limit had been reached before Pavlova's appearance. And yet there again Pavlova asserted her supremacy. None of her predecessors can bear comparison with her. For instance, she accomplished all technical feats as easily as Leniani : but Leniani, when dancing, remains cold, deliberate, mechanical; and sometimes one sees that she uses exertion. Here virtuosity appertains to the Italian tradition, which has led dancing perilously near the line where art ends and acrobacy begins. Pavlova's technique does not predetermine her dancing, but seems to take its rise as she dances. It is live, warm, and spirited. It is instinct with compelling sincerity. The spectators remain unaware of it until her dance comes to a close, when they suddenly realise the extent of technical difficulties, concealed by the supreme beauty of the execution, that have entered into the composition of what she has just achieved.

The foregoing brief description of Pavlova's artistic endowments shows why she acquired her supreme rank among all the choregraphic stars of the whole world. We have followed in their evolution the three main elements of her genius : her aerial buoyancy and grace, her perfect technique, her power for dramatic expression. The combination of those three elements is to be found in no other dancer. Any one of them would suffice to enable a dancer to range high among her rivals : but when nature has endowed one woman with all three, that woman stands out as a wonder. A well-known art critic, after having seen Pavlova dance on the stage of the Theatre des Champs-Elysées, spoke in the following terms to a number of young artists who had mustered around him :

" Study that woman closely, young men. She is not a mere

ANNA PAVLOVA
dans « Le Cygne »

woman; she is an art gallery, a vast gallery of attitudes, of lines, of ideas plastically expressed; she is the soul of gesture and movement. Each one of her movements deserves to be embodied in a drawing, or in a modelling, and perpetuated as a teaching for future generations ".

Indeed, Pavlova is neither a Taglioni, nor a Leniani, nor a Pucchi. Taglioni was endowed with lightness, but deficient in technique. Pucchi had dramatic power, but her dancing lacked beauty. Leniani possessed an excellent technique, but fell short in pantomimic expression. There is but one Pavlova, in whom the soul of dancing has found its complete expression. And that is why Pavlova is a dancer of genius.

IV

It his famous play *La Nouvelle Idole*, François de Curel puts in doctor Cormier's mouth a declaration to the effect that five hundred years hence, science will know what the human soul actually is. When psychological science finds its true basis, we shall know " whether it is immortal, whence it comes, whither it goes. And whoever descants upon judgment, imagination, memory, and will, shall make use of data free from any element of uncertainty." Then, perhaps, we shall know what genius consists of. But up to now, no thinker has proved capable of supplying a satisfactory definition of its essence and nature. Five hundred years hence, if we are to believe François de Curel's hero, our descendents will be in a position accurately to define the nature of genius; to understand, for instance, how it came to pass that an artist such as Taglioni, who was neither beautiful nor shapely, should have stood so high in the opinion of her public. Taglioni's features were irregular, her complexion was sallow. Her arms were so disproportionately long that her father, a ballet-master, invented for her a special posture of the arms, teaching her how to fold them so as to conceal that defect. Pavlova's features are lovely and soulful, her figure is delicate and shapely; but many are the dancers who, though lacking neither beauty nor shapeliness, never achieve an artistic success.

A great deal has been written about Pavlova. And a great deal more remains to be written, for her wonderful and surpassing genius is not on the wane, has not even come to a standstill; it is asserting itself fully, and more powerfully than ever. She is not one of those artists whose talent can be submitted to an analysis after completing which one can say to the public : " Here are her merits, there her shortcomings. Deduct the lesser quantity from the greater, and you will know what to think of her ".

Indeed crude methods of that kind — although certain critics will resort to them — are perfectly useless. Pavlova must be considered as a whole, as the indescribable manifestation of something that we can neither understand or define. Analysis would be worse than useless. The flame radiating from the very core of all her conceptions and illuminating her acting, her attitudes, and her dancing, is the pure flame of genius. And that much the enraptured public realises and rejoices in. Pavlova has toured all over the world, and conquered audiences of all races and temperaments. It is therefore superfluous to describe in all their constituent parts her various attitudes, steps, movements, or any other point referring to her technique. Let it suffice to mention their buoyancy, their grace, their finish and aerial imponderability, their perfect beauty and elegance in lines, colour and style, their perfect coordination in one general scheme. They delight not by virtue of the effect of this point or that, but by the perfect fusion of all elements in one great harmonious whole. She does not merely dance : she creates, she sets up arrays of pictures before the spectators' eyes. Let us adduce a few instances.

When she comes, one has the feeling of witnessing a mysterious and magic transformation : one feels that what Maeterlinck, in " the Blue Bird ", has called " the soul of souless things ", may indeed exist somewhere, far away in the realms of winds and snow. And it is that small, shimmering soul that makes us believe in the tale so tellingly, so poetically unfolded by the dance-fairy. A simple classical " turn " has become an inspired and lofty work of art. Take, again, Liszt's *Preludes,* founded on Lamartine's philosophical and poetical saying : " What is our life but a series of preludes to that unknown tune which death strikes up?" In his tone-poem, the composer has achieved a perfect union of the poetic principle and of music. And the concrete physical expression of Lamartine's idea, translated by Liszt into sounds and rhythms, is in turn translated by Pavlova into plastic imagery. And from her skilful, intricate dancing, a figure suddenly disengages itself, the

Photo Ira Hill.

PAVLOVA
IN " THE DRAGON-FLY "

figure of the Dream-Woman, the figure that Botticelli has often evoked in his subtle, visionary pictures.

And as regards Saint-Saens's *La Mort du Cygne*, what can one say that has not already been said? That scene is Pavlova's own creation. In her wake, practically every dancer has tried her fortune with that *Mort du Cygne*. But Pavlova remains the inventor and the greatest exponent of that delightful gem of choregraphy. The Swan's song interpreted by her becomes a picture in which are combined romantic elements of the kind that suit her so wonderfully. Her delicate, frail figure, her pathetic grace, so preraphaelite in character, the grief in her eyes, all that, in a setting of moonlight and to the soft music of 'cellos and harps, constitues a vision of ineffable beauty.

Remembering all those classical achievements of hers, one wonders all the more to see her appear in the character of an Oriental dancer, glowing with passion, in her *Syrian dance,* a masterpiece of ethnographical dancing.

Pavlova's wonderful impersonations and creations will be referred to more fully in another chapter; if I have mentioned a few here, it is only by way of illustrations.

A talent that reaches far and deep, as versatile as it is great; now a pearl of tender lustre, now a diamond of dazzling glow. Indeed it was not without full reason that Paris, where all the famous dancers of all times have appeared, should have said of Pavlova, through the mouth of its leading art critics : " She is the greatest dancer that has ever been. "

V

In the introductory chapter, I have referred to the importance of classical technique in the art of the Ballet.

In all arts, technique is the material which the maker of the work of art utilises. Therefore, it is impossible to dispense here with a description of Pavlova's stupendous technique in classical dancing. Whoever had remained some time without seeing her was thoroughly unprepared to find in her so great an exponent of classical technique — the greatest exponent, indeed, that has ever appeared on any stage, as I have said before.

One had never seen before the most complicated pirouettes executed in so accurate and so impeccably finished in style. There is no other dancer capable of "*pizzicati* on tip-toe" so clear-cut, so elegant and so flowing, nor one who can display a similar firmness in what the old terminology described as "toes of steel". Her long pauses on tip-toe are amazing. One would hardly believe them possible ; and when one sees them, one hardly trusts one's eyes. Her balance, again, is something to marvel at, and almost appears to exceed the bounds of possibility.

The transcending merit and charm of Pavlova's technique lie in the fact that, although this technique is superior to that of any other dancer, Pavlova, even when engaged in supreme feats of virtuosity and *bravura*, preserves all her spontaneity and ease. We know many choregraphic stars, mentioned in previous chapters, who can accomplish the most difficult evolutions and steps. But they could not avoid revealing the effort, sacrificing something of the beauty of movements and attitudes, of the coordination between arms, legs, torso, and head. So that, taking one thing with another, that wealth of technique not only failed to be a source of artistic enjoyment, but became repulsive, on account of its obviously laboured character and wastage of physical energy. Pavlova, on the contrary, does amazingly difficult things without the onlookers ever experiencing anxiety, even for a fraction of a second, or even realising the difficulties she is toying with. All is done smoothly, elegantly, with perfect ease. One admires the beauty of her "ports de bras", the suppleness of her body, the subtlety and expressiveness of her legs and feet, her sensitive, wistful, head — in short, the whole of her person, marvelously slim and elusive, moves with perfectly coordinated harmony ; and to the onlookers, even the most difficult threefold pirouette — a feat never accomplished before — or long pause on tip-toe (which constitues a miracle of balance) appear as mere play, no less natural than all her picturesque arabesques or attitudes.

Leniani, the exponent *par excellence* of modern virtuosity, surprised by her technique without delighting. Pavlova's technique both surprises and delights. But, as I have said before, to submit the dancing of that inspired and unique artist to a bald analysis would be highly unprofitable. This dancing must be freely enjoyed ; and one should feel grateful that our time should have given to the world an artist so surpassing in genius. The uninitiated to the secrets of choregraphy remain unaware of Pavlova's peerless tech-

PAVLOVA
IN " THE RUSSIAN DANCE "

nique : and that is the highest tribute that could be paid to it.
Indeed, even in her most difficult adagios or variations, technique
ceases to exist. She has so perfect a command of it, that she succeeds
in hiding it from the onlookers' eyes. No one could notice at which
particular instant she is accomplishing some unusually difficult feat.
One sees her, one witnesses wonderful results : but the mechanism of the execution remains concealed, there is nothing to reveal
the springs and the labour which produce any particular action.
Technical creation can reach no higher level. When technique
is so absolutely perfect, it ceases to be a thing that only connoisseurs are capable of appreciating. It becomes accessible and
intelligible to all, especially when the dancer does not sacrifice to

it anything of her native grace and elegance, nor of the meaning of her performance.

In music, harmony is produced by a simultaneity of simple sounds, melody by their succession in time. Dancing is the visible expression of the soul of music, of its rhythms translated into rhythms in space. The aesthetic impression conveyed by a rhythmical succession of sounds depends not only upon the relative duration of the sounds, but also upon the accents and phrasing. Likewise, in dancing, the succession of the units, or beats, remains non-rhythmical if it lacks proper accents. In the static arts symmetry, in the dynamic arts rhythm, produce an artistic impression only if the various details are merged in to one general unity. From that point of view, Pavlova's dancing is something unique, and sets a wonderful example. Each of its technical components, each of the choregraphic figures in which they are grouped, are linked together in one general rhythmic scheme which closely corresponds to the emotional purport. In each of her poses, in each of her attitudes, that function of rhythm plainly asserts itself; and the most complex and difficult things give the impression of flowing ease and grace — simply because movements and attitudes follow one another in perfectly eurhythmic order, and the accents are perfectly distinct and balanced.

The sense of rhythm, of the rhythm consisting in the repetition of an action at well-regulated intervals, although inborn in man and bearing upon his mental organisation as well as the physical, does not form part of every dancer's equipment. Given, for instance, a variation in 6/8 tempo, if a dancer contents herself with executing six movements to each bar, without realising where the accents fall, there can be no question of true rhythm.

The sense of rhythm in dancing is something very complex; or, more properly speaking, constitutes a special and exceptional gift. It is not uncommon to see a dancer endowed with a keen musical ear, and capable of repeating a tune correctly and easily after having heard it but once, and nevertheless incapable of dancing rhythmically. In Pavlova, the sense of rhythm is developed to the utmost. In her artist soul rhythm lives its own independent life. She may be unaware that a swan in flight gives two strokes of its wings per second, and a dragon-fly twenty-eight. But look at her executing *The Swan's death* or *The Dragon-Flies,* and you will realise what her inborn, organic sense of rhythm is. Instinctively, she coordinates the rhythmic action of dancing with the inner rhythm of movement, and achieves a total assimilation between the two. There may be cases when, if the inner autonomy of rhythm is to be acknowledged, that fusion is impracticable : but then Pavlova, intuitively, strives at least to ensure the coincidence of the stresses or accents of both rhythms : in other words, she establishes a simple relation between the inner, artistic rhythm, and the outer, physical rhythm. And this affords the explanation why she conveys such an intensity and depth of aesthetic emotion; it is the very principle and secret of her art and temperament.

The question of grace is in close connexion with the question of rhythm. Should dancing be submitted to all the restrictions consequent upon too narrow a conception of rhythm, it would lose all its grace. An excess of meticulous accuracy would result in making dancing appear purely mechanical, automatic. Hence the anti-artistic character of steps such as *fouettés* or *jetés en tournant* when executed merely by way of displaying virtuosity. Independence of rhythm in movements, which nothing but the dictates of the indefinable inner aesthetic sense should govern, is a condition *sine qua non* of grace in dancing. Another necessary condition of grace is the full command of all technicalities, so that the dancer may freely give the rein to her imagination and moods. In an artist such as Pavlova, whose mastery of the complexities and subtleties of modern classical technique is unrivalled, the temperament enjoys its full scope, because it is unrestricted by any shortcoming in physical proficiency. Hence, a surpassing intensity and expressiveness in Pavlova's grace and beauty when dancing. By way of illustration, let it suffice to recall the frolicsome, humorous coquetry, the spontaneous glee, the fiery temperament she displays in the *Syrian Dance.*

VI

Nowadays, the technique of classical dancing has become something very elaborate, each detail of which has been thoroughly considered, and settled practically once for all. Yet, of course, the individual temperament of an artist may lead to certain predilections, to a particular conception of one technical element or another, to a special application of this resource or that in dancing.

The steadfast foundation of to-day's classical dancing is supplied by five positions, out of which the whole of modern practice has evolved. They were established at the beginning of the eighteenth century by Feuillet. The Italian Ballet-master Magri enumerates twenty positions. Noverre (1727-1809), the father of the modern Ballet, repudiated the principle of fundamental positions, asserting that to stipulate exactly how far apart a dancer's feet should be placed, how high they should be raised, and how narrow or ample each curve they describe should be, etc. was incompatible with artistic dancing. He declared that in dancing, everything was a matter of each dancer's taste and physical structure.

Time and experience, however, have proved that Feuillet was in the right. His five positions have remained the basis of classical dancing. Of the five, the third used to be considered as the most natural and graceful, the fifth as the most elaborate and tense. From the beginning of the nineteenth century, however, that fifth position assumed prominent importance. The five positions of the arms were also maintained. The same may be said of the various technical steps : some became the fashion and were misused, others were set aside and sank into oblivion.

The modern school, in the course of it long process of evolution, has derived from those five original positions a great quantity of technical steps, which in time increased in complexity as well as in number. Every step gave birth to another step, which in turn served to introduce another, more complicated. And a good teacher follows the very same order of progression, so as to ensure the gradual and logical training of his pupils. At lesson-time, the good teacher may and should prescribe the hardest tasks and exercises, not excluding purely acrobatic *tours de force*. In that respect, even the *fouettés* may be useful (in order to increase the steadiness of the balance and the coordination of movements), even the so-called *grand écart* (as a gymnastic exercise which improves the working of an insufficiently trained hip-joint). The old Ballet-masters' and the dancers of the Italian school's mistake was simply to introduce these school-exercices into their stage-dancing, to think they could be made to serve the purposes of art. That constituted an offence against the sense of logic as well as against the aesthetic sense. Those dancers' object was solely to astonish the public by their virtuosity, which they carried to the utmost possible limits.

Pavlova's greatest achievement is that she realised that to proceed thus was to sin against the very spirit of art. Endowed with a complete mastery of school technique, she nevertheless discarded all that had its place in school training but was incompatible with artistic dancing on the stage. And that is the reason why in her dancing, which remains instinct with the purest and best traditions of the classical school, all appears so simple, so natural, as grateful to the eye as the dances of old Greece. She has never condescended to resort to the meretricious technical tricks that rouse the lesser educated fraction of an audience to frantic but cheap applause.

One may say, without exaggerating, that she has created a technique of her own, a " Pavlova-technique ", exactly as Rembrandt has created his technique of the chiaroscuro.

If we owe to Camargo the *entrechat* and to Heinel the *pirouette*, to Pavlova we are indebted for precious innovations in technique: the trill on the points, and the long pause on the points, both wonderfully beautiful. Her *pirouettes* are something apart and unequalled for boldness, accuracy and beauty.

There exist a great number of theories of the *pirouette*. That put forth by Blasis, which is founded upon mathematical principles and describes how the body maintains its centre of gravity unaltered while the circular motion is being performed, has been accepted as, and remains, classical.

Pavlova's pirouettes are altogether impulsive, elemental; they come like so many flashes, unheralded by the stereotyped preparatory position (*préparation à la pirouette*) with its *plié* and gathering of momentum by that swinging of the arms to which so many dancers resort inartistically and crudely. With Pavlova, it seems as though some internal, spiritual power impels her to enhance her dancing with that brilliant arabesque.

The steps composed by her comprise neither meretricious and mechanical *fouettés*, nor acrobatic *jetés en tournant*, nor the cynical *grand écart* dear to the music-hall stage. And that, I think, is the reason why some people cannot fully comprehend the significance and beauty of her art. That art is too subtle, too aristocratic — as indeed all genuine art is — to be accessible to the mass of ordinary theatre-goers.

I do not mean to imply that her art does not prove attractive to the masses. Quite on the contrary, her overwhelming successes in Paris, before crowded halls, suffice to prove that her dancing does hold the general public spell-bound. But irresponsible enthusiasm and genuinely enlightened appreciation are two very different things. It is my belief that the subtleties of her art remain — and will

PAVLOVA
IN THE " BACCHANAL "

long remain — unperceived by a considerable fraction of the public.

The question of the democratisation of art is exceedingly complex. Can art, which in its very essence is — and in my opinion will always be — aristocratic, that is, the apanage of the elect few, really be made democratic? Is it suitable to bring it out of its temple into the streets, and to make it the apanage of the multitude? There have always been genius on one hand, the multitude on the other, with an abyss between the two — although often genius has arisen from the very midst of the multitude. Creative artists are few. They create, not for the sake of the multitude, but because their creative instinct impels them, and must find its outlet. Of all psychological processes, the process of creation is the most recondite and wonderful. A symphony conceived by the soul of an artist, the product of his deepest feeling, elaborately worked out in its proportions, flow, and setting for the various components of the orchestra that will execute it, can hardly be democratised, if the word is to mean made accessible to the many who lack all notions of rhythm, tempo, harmony, counterpoint and other fundamental elements of music. Only people who have received at least a modicum of musical culture, or who are gifted with a sense for music, will realise the full beauty of its purport, and understand the full technical process of musical creation. For that reason music will never be for the *profanum vulgus*. When a tune becomes what is called popular, a thing that the masses rejoice in, it means that it is no longer capable of appealing to the educated taste. It means that the times have outlived that particular type of music; and at that very moment, the genuine musicians, the elect, are busily creating new types which remain inaccessible and unintelligible to the throng. Art stands jealously aloof from the crowd. Intent upon preserving its purity undefiled, it keeps to the heights. For instance, no sooner had Italian music stepped out of the temple of art, the theatre, into the street ; no sooner were the tunes from *Traviata* on the lips of workmen and kitchen-wenches, that Wagner appeared and raised art to a new level, so high that it seemed out of reach.

And when Wagner in turn descends from the summits into the main road, ceases to be a mysterious demi-god, then another genius will forthwith appear who will reinstate music into a jealously guarded temple.

Certain moralists have asserted that music must be democratised, because it has a beneficient moral influence. But what of Nero, who played the lyre whilst gloating upon the sufferings of the thousands victims burning to death when to gratify his whim Rome was set on fire? Let art, then, remain on its pinnacle, and the crowd pay a humble and reverent homage to it. There is no lack of established forms, the legacy of the past, which in the natural course of things have become the apanage of the multitude.

In old Greece, there existed a number of folk-dances, most of them licentious in character — for instance the Phallophoria; but only the initiated participated in the dancing that formed part of the Delphic mysteries. Primitive folk-dances belong to the people, and remain within the scope of the people's understanding; whereas they find an elaborately conceived and skilfully executed Ballet-Variation or Adagio difficult to understand, and in the long run wearisome. Only the genius of a Pavlova can command towards the higher technicalities of dancing the attention of a mass that knows nothing about them. In that respect, her power is unique, and is the result of the fact that her surpassing technique serves one sole purpose : genuine expression of what each dance is meant to express. Her art, in all things, is supremely human.

VII

When speaking of Pavlova in connexion with the classical Ballet, special mention should be made of her striking creative power in the province of mimic action. For during the past decade, the tendency of the Ballet to become a choregraphic drama has asserted itself more and more strongly.

Noverre himself used to dream of dramatising dancing, but in vain. He has written volumes on that topic. But he was too far in advance of his times, and his voice remained the *vox clamans in deserto*. Far more, whenever he composed or produced a Ballet, either through lack of capacity or through lack of resources, he never succeeded in carrying his theories into practice. The transition from Ballet-Divertissement to dramatic Ballet, from the conventional mask to the free play of live features, was insufficiently prepared. Obviously, evolution in art must be gradual, as is evolution in nature : otherwise it would be not evolution, that is, development, but revolution, that is, subversion. A revolution, however successful in its time, must needs lead to a reaction, a return to the point at which

Photo S. Bransburg.

PAVLOVA
IN " THE DYING ROSE "

the subversion of traditions established by centuries of evolution had started. It is the law—the law of revolutions.

The evolution from the mere display of dancing in the shape of a Divertissement to the choregraphic drama, replete with meaning, foreshadowed by Noverre, remained very gradual, and was completed in the 'thirties, at the time when the Romantic movement started.

The Romantic period, which in art last about thirty years (1820-1850) opened with the publication of Lamartine's *Méditations*. It is upon the stage that it exercised the greatest influence and found its fullest expression. Later, when referring to *Giselle*, I shall deal with its artistic doctrines and principally with their application to the Ballet.

The progress of the Ballet has remained closely bound with that of literature, an art whose tendencies, in proportion as they assert themselves, find in choregraphy their true reflection. The Ballet has paid its tribute to pseudo-classicism : all Ballets prior to Noverre, and even those of Noverre and Didelot, are cases in point. The subjects are borrowed from old mythologies; their cast consists of gods, demi-gods, and heroes. To Romanticism we owe the *Sylphides*, *Giselle*, and *The enchanted Lake*, besides a great number of less famous Ballets. The birth of nationalism in art gave rise, in various countries, to Ballets whose subjects were borrowed from national life or national lore. Impressionnism, and the return to favour of antiquity, resulted in the Ballets of Fokin and Gorski. Cubism and futurism gave us Nijinski's and Miassin's. And perhaps Dadaism, that latest of innovations, will have upon the Ballet a temporary repercussion.

We always see the Ballet borrowing its inspiration from the works of prominent writers, such as Victor Hugo *(Esmeralda)*, Heine and Théophile Gautier *(Giselle)*, Perrault *(The Sleeping Beauty)*, Byron *(The Corsair)*, Oscar Wilde *(The tragedy of Salomé)*, Hoffman *(Coppélia)* not to mention many others.

When in Western Europe the tendency cropped up to do away with all "literature" proper — that tendency which has played havoc with the stage-play as generally conceived — the Ballet followed suit, and tried to do without "literature": that is, without plot or "programme", and to rely solely upon plastic effects and expression. Thus did Fokin compose les *Sylphides*, a Ballet with neither subject nor characters, consisting merely in a choregraphic interpretation of the music's moods and emotions — an array of garlands and posies of melodies and dances, poetry for the sake of poetry and dancing for the sake of dancing.

Now let us revert to the time when the Ballet, ceasing to be a mere Divertissement, first assumed a dramatic character. In Ballets such as *The Dancing Girl, Esmeralda, Giselle*, not dancing only, but acting was necessary. And there could be no question of acting on one hand, and dancing on the other hand : the dancing had to be dramatic, and the pantomimic acting to be imbued with plastic qualities. When the dancing-girl is suddenly bitten by the snake; when Esmeralda, tortured by jealousy, is compelled to dance before the man who has deceived her and his *fiancée;* when Giselle pitifully dances, remembering even in her insanity the happy days forever gone — dancing *per se* is inadequate : the situations call for live dramatic colour and expression in every step.

In such cases, the dancer must possess the gift for dramatic expression. I have already mentioned Pucchi, Kshessinska, Preobrajenska, and others endowed with that gift. But Pavlova, who can be compared only with the great Duse, stands apart and unequalled in the galaxy of dancers who are also mimes. Her dramatic talent owes its special depth and intensity to a particular kind of mysticism which hardly comes within the scope of the ordinary methods of critical analysis. For her genius is not divided into air-tight compartments : it is one harmonious whole whose technical elements are wonderfully blended and merged into one another, indiscerptible even for the purposes of analysis.

What she gives is neither pathos and tragedy as understood in olden times, nor the naturalism and realism of the Russian school. It is something apart, which belongs to her alone, the very emanation of her soul. It is pathos perhaps, but lyrical, tender and dreamy. Also, perhaps, realism, but tinged by her with a poetry that is purely subjective. It is a series of realistic elements transmuted and reflected in the wonderful prism of her soul, whose radiation emblasons them with the softest, brightest colours in endless variety.

In dramatic moments, as when dancing, all that she does is imponderable, elemental, perspicuous; it is romanticism, but a romanticism as full of action as of passion, spirited even in affliction, free from the conventional exaggerations in fashion in the 'thirties.

It is difficult to explain the methods by which she achieves that wonderful intensity of dramatic expression, and moves her audiences so deeply. The onlooker can no more discover the workings of her dramatic performances than he can discuss the part played by sheer technique in her classical dancing. The stage is not unlike a magnifying glass. The artificial rays of the foot-lights, the convergence

Héliog. Schützenberger. Paris.

LA MORT DU CYGNE

d'après le tableau de Sir John Lavery

of dialogue, movements and action, are so many elements tending to concentrate the images of life or of fancy within the smallest of compasses. Everything that takes place on the stage tends towards exaggeration. Colours are louder, gestures sharper, tears more burning, laughter more obstreperous. A wide range of emotions has to be condensed into a scene lasting perhaps a couple of minutes; the events of a whole day will be crowded into an act whose duration does not exceed twenty minutes. Moreover, all must appear probable to the spectator, whether the play be founded upon actual life or upon purely poetic fancy. If that essential condition is ignored, if there are any errors in the conventional distribution and conduct of the action, the play will appear, as the case may be, intolerably artificial or inordinately crude.

For all those reasons, the artist stands in need of great discriminative power and a keen sense of proportion. His conception of each part he plays must be circumscribed, so to speak, by a circle marking the limit which his pathos, however great the emotion that inspires his acting, should under no conditions overstep. He must constantly remember the existence of the soft pedal, and avail himself of it freely. The misuse of the loud pedal is as bad and inartistic in acting as in music. One might compare the results with those of photography, remembering how all the idiosyncrasies of the features are emphasised in the negative plate — so that in order to obtain a good portrait, it is necessary to resort to retouching.

Film-actors are well aware of that particularity of the camera, and therefore restrain their gestures and the play of their features correspondingly. At times, a talented actor will adequately express the deepest of emotions or passions by a barely perceptible twitch of one of the muscles of the face. Pavlova, the great interpreter of tragedies, resorts to the same sober and simple methods. The old Greeks refrained from frantic gesticulation and from shouting : their gestures and tone were suggestive of pathos, but not graphic. And it is in Greek tragedy that we find the highest expression of human pathos. Self-control is in fact the essential condition of the actor's power to communicate emotion.

Let us remember Pavlova's acting in *The Dancing-Girl*, in *Amaryllis*, in *Giselle :* then, having analysed her dramatic methods, we cannot fail to realise how very simple, quiet and subdued they are. That is the artist's retouching, which imparts ineffable charm to a picture artistically conceived and adequately carried out. Pavlova is aware of the line of demarcation that separates artistic truth from mundane falsehood; and can artistic truth be the result of a convention? However, the paradox will baffle none but those people who lack the sense of stage-conditions. The apparent simplicity and spontaneity of Pavlova's acting are naturally the result of the formidable amount of labour she has devoted to the technique of her art; a labour that fortunately remains unrevealed to the onlooker. But alone an artist of surpassing merit and talent is able to show such results for her labour.

VIII

In the Ballet, as in every other art-form, style must ever be present. There is no true art where true style is lacking. Style is the atmosphere of the period reflected in art. Every great art period has its own atmosphere, which constitutes its style.

This style consists of elements that are pratically imponderable, of moods and inclinations hardly perceptible to contemporaries. All of them born out of the depths of the people's spirit, these moods seek their outlet in outer forms correponding to the idiosyncrasies of the people's aesthetic feeling. Primitive, unconscious artists coordinate those lines, dashes and curves into some kind of primitive arabesque, rudimentary song or artless dance.

Style, as all things, is subject to evolution, in the course of which it is improved and enriched. After the unconscious, purely intuitive artists, others appear, more enlightened and more experienced. They start to elaborate the primitive elements of the people's creation, to build them up into more complex works. The original tunes of a period remain unaltered, but acquire a deeper artistic meaning and greater finish from the material point of view.

Style is always the result of the reciprocal influences of time and circumstances: the race and customs of a people, geographical and historical conditions, the climate. Spanish dances comprise many broken lines, abrupt movements and *positions cambrées*: those idiosyncrasies constitue the ordained style of Spanish dancing, a style that is the emanation of a Southern temperament and of the fiery climate, a style whose chiaroscuro is as rich in sharp contrasts as a Spanish landscape is, with its deep blue sky against which buildings stand out in strong relief in the sunshine.

In the folk-dances of Great-Russia we find neither such angles, nor such breaks. Similar to the country's scenery, they are essentially quiet et even; their movements are slow. There the sun is pale, the country flat; the atmosphere blurs contours, attenuates contrasts and does not foster warmth of temperament. Hence the evenness, slowness and quietness of the dances. The chief character of the Spanish dances is their design and pattern; that of Great Russia's dances, their colour-scheme and lack of definite lines.

Few are the artists to whom it is given to identify themselves soul and body with the style of every production they appear in. And no stage has ever possessed another artist such as Pavlova, whose sense of style and gift for style are unique. There have been and are many dancers who are capable of imparting the appearance of style to their dancing. But the appearance only; an appearance that is the result of their artifice. And in art, anything artificial, anything insincere is doomed to failure, and will never satisfy the aesthetic sense.

Pavlova's artistic temperament is so deeply imbued with the rarest and truest sense of style, that as soon as she has donned the garb belonging to a period, she becomes the perfect picture of a woman of that period; and one finds it hard to believe that she is not really all that she impersonates.

I am not referring to the mere outward appearances of style. With the aid of make-up, wigs, properties and costume, and by resorting to a number of attitudes, gestures and other mannerisms established by theatrical conventions, any normally gifted artist can give a fair representment of any style. But none of these resources will help to bring him any nearer the genuine spirit that will make that style live, nor enable him to penetrate the secrets of bygone times, to achieve the wonderful and unique results to which Pavlova has accustomed us. Her *Giselle* is no copy of some painting or engraving, but indeed the very maiden whose story is being set forth to us. That genuineness of her impersonation of the simple dreamy peasant maid gives the lie to her conventional attire. The impersonation is romantic : but the romantic character of her acting is the sum total of an infinity of small traits which become merged into one harmonious whole, giving the very synthesis of the period's style, in the spirit and not only superficially. It is in that respect that she stands supreme among artists.

There is no resemblance between the timid, quiet maiden, so pathetic in her harrowing distress, that she is as Giselle, and the fiery Oriental of the *Syrian Dance*, whose fondness for adornment gains the upper hand over all other feelings. It is not her attire only, but her movements, now languidly impassioned, now eager and fervid; the play of her features; her contemptuous smiles, her glances, her wiles. The East is before us in its fulness. In the true atmosphere of the hareem, the girl slave exercises her power over the man her master.

In the Louis XIV Minuet, Pavlova avails herself with infinite skill and most aptly of the quaint and elaborate attitudes, motions, curtsies, and other mannerisms of the period — not as one who has merely consumed the midnight oil might do, but as a genuine artist who understands and loves that period, and lives the life expressed in that bygone style. It is no copy one beholds, but an actual seventeenth century marchioness; one feels that she was exactly thus and could not have been other.

So great is the sway of her marvelous genius.

The French have a particular admiration for style in art. One of the foremost Parisian critics, M. Jean-Louis Vaudoyer, has paid to Pavlova's gift for style the following tribute:

" We preserve a live and grateful memory of Pavlova's wonderful art, of her surpassing grace. We must say that very seldom a dancer has given us so great a feeling of style. Her style, indeed, is a magic combination of most variform qualities harmoniously and symmetrically developed, and perfectly blended together. It imparts not only artistic emotion, but a sense of perpetuity. It ignores ephemeral fashions, and does not mirror the mere conceits and mannerisms of a given period. It is the style which enables an artist — be she actress, or singer, or dancer — to usher us into an ideal abode in the Elysian Fields of art. By virtue of that priceless gift, those artists can make pristine and conventional things so live that they will move us to tears. These artists are not the bearers of new messages : they are the classics. They reveal to us perfect beauty and magnify it, reviving aspects of it that had died out and were forgotten. Pavlova is as great in dancing as Racine in poetry, Poussin in painting, Gluck in music. A few steps, a few motions of her hands, an inclination of her head, a smile, and suddenly we behold in the very flesh now Niobe mourning her children, now Terpsichore herself, leading with Apollo the dance on the slopes of the Sacred Hill. "

In the above lines, the writer has most aptly defined the very spirit of classicism, that quality so mysterious and yet so definite, which comes as the crowning grace of all other qualities which go to

Photo Van Riel.

PAVLOVA AND STOWITZ
IN THE "SYRIAN DANCE"

the making of great works of art.   As he points out, classicism resides
indeed in those elements of universal and eternal beauty, independent of ephemeral fashions, conceits and mannerisms of any given

period, whose live presence we acknowledge in all true masterpieces, ancient and modern, be they obviously " classical " in tendencies and character, or be they of the sort which we naturally incline to define as " romantic ". And again style, that most elusive and yet most needful of the qualities which artists, whether they be creators or mere interpreters, must be endowed with if they are to be great in their art, resides chiefly, if not solely, in the capacity to disengage and to coordinate those elements, so as to remain faithful to all conditions of race, period and setting, whilst avoiding to yield to their influence slavishly. A perfect balance between what, in a work of art, is universal and eternal, and what is but topical and transient, is the ideal towards which all conscientious and genuine artists strive : but few are those who actually achieve it, and achieve it so convincingly, that all judges agree in praising their achievement without restriction.

Pavlova has intuitively, and from the very outset of her career, directed her efforts towards the conquest of that lofty ideal. Gifted as she is, and feeling as she does, she could hardly be conceived as doing otherwise. Whether after having seen her incarnations of the various aspects of classical beauty in choregraphy we shall agree with Vaudoyer's in saying that an artist who can rise to so high a level is the bearer of no new message, may perhaps be doubted. For instinctively we speak of her dancing as a revelation; and we feel that the term is true, that the perfect cooperation of feeling, intelligence, sense of proportion, of fitness and of beauty, has created something which comes to us for the first time in all its peerless radiance.

IX

I have striven, by describing Pavlova in the spirit, to show that in truth she is the greatest of choregraphic artists. As often as not, critical analysis remains powerless to deal with the nature and essence of so rare a thing as genius. We may indeed establish that she is the most aerial of dancers; that in her technique she displays surpassing virtuosity, whilst never giving any impression of difficulty nor of labour; that as regards pantomime and dramatic expression, she is on a par with the greatest of tragedians; that she is endowed

PAVLOVA
Taking a lesson with the Maestro Cecchetti

with the fullest and truest sense of rhythm, that the beauty of her deportment is wonderful, that in her dancing and acting the very loftiest tradition and a perfectly aristocratic quality are asserted and sustained; and that she possesses an unerring sense of proportion and a genius for style. But to explain how these several invaluable assets merge into one whole; to define the process and laws through which the genius of that most extraordinary dancer of our time asserts itself; to make clear the actual mechanism of her achievements — all that is hardly within the pale of critical analysis.

Yet again, is it so very necessary to do it at all? Are not those profound emotions, those grateful thrills, those wonderful delights that we owe her convincing enough? They are indeed for all who know her and duly admire her genius. But for all those who neither have seen her nor shall see her, a critical analysis and some kind of positive statement are necessary.

Let us remember the words quoted in a foregoing chapter: " She is not a mere woman : she embodies a whole art-gallery of attitudes, of lines, of plastically expressed thought, of the very spirit of acting. Every one of her motions should be recorded in a design or in a statue, for the education of posterity. "

A record of the various manifestations of her genius will supply future generations with a wealth of precious materials. In that respect, the cinematograph might prove useful : not the usual type, but one capable of faithfully reproducing rhythm, all movements remaining closely bound with the accompanying music. That kind of cinematograph, unfortunately, has yet to be invented.

I shall conclude this chapter by quoting the words of M. Roger-Ducos, a French critic who in 1920 published in *Le Carnet de la Semaine* the following terse and exhaustive description of Pavlova's rank in art :

" One should apply no epithets to her : for she is *The Dancer*. Does the art of which she is a priestess include any desirable thing that she lacks, or has not fully mastered? All criticism collapses, save the criticism of enthusiasm.

" She is endowed with nobility of features and mien, beauty of carriage, shapely arms, a waist supple and slender, legs whose conformation reveal both grace and power.

" She commands expressiveness, sweetness, and strength, elegance and purity, profundity and accuracy; never does she stray from truth, nor indulge in wanton vagaries. Her acting is instinct

Photo Goyzueta.

PAVLOVA
IN THE " TAMBOURINE "

with poetry, constitutes a wonderful blend of pathos and humour, versatile and soulful.

" She controls her genius even when she seens to yield to its impulses ; and it is impossible to discern what subtle magic enables her dancing to interpret, down to its utmost depth, not only the composer's motives, but also the inspiration in which the libretto originated.

" Her dancing seems to be thought cast into its natural mould, splendour enhanced with something that belongs to eternity. Whether to an audience of connoisseurs or in front of the most unin- itiated and refractory crowd, let her dance *the Swan's Death* or *Giselle*, and all will be delighted, thrilled, moved to the very core.

" What she dances she speaks, and speaks in most wonderful language.

" Her feet are as light as wings, her rhythm speaks of dreams entrancing, her expressiveness outruns fancy.

" She is the Dancer, she is Dance itself. "

ANNA PAVLOVA

Жизель
ПАВЛОВА
(отдѣлка бѣлыми)

BAKST

Water-Colour drawing for Giselle's costume
by Léon Bakst

« GISELLE »

I

GISELLE is, of all Pavlova's creations, the most wonderful, the most comprehensive, and deserves most special consideration.

Giselle has revealed her genius in its true light, showing to the full her creative imagination and the versatility of her talent. With her interpretation of that work, she arose to outstanding fame, and added her name to those of the most famous dancers in the annals of the stage. Therefore, we select that one work out of the whole of her repertoire, and shall dwell on it a while.

Giselle was first produced during the 'forties, the very heart of the romantic period, whose influence upon poetry and the stage has been so great under the acknowledged leadership of Victor Hugo. Romanticism started to do away with the tenets of a classicism intent upon deriving inspiration from the old world, and solely concerned

with the " lofty ", the " beautiful ", and " common sense ". Romanti-
cisme did not shun life, even in its lurid aspects. It began to derive
its materials, not from pagan mythology, but from the middle-ages,
substituting for the heroes of antiquity characters, not absolutely
familiar, yet more accessible to us in their bearing and passions.

The Romanticis devoted their utmost energy to the reform of the
stage, introducing greater unity, more scope for imagination, a new
sense of intimacy, and a greater freedom in the very conception of the
drama. They did away with the dead-weight of classical formule ;
and, having cleared the ground of the more obtrusive conventions,
opened the stage to both the fantastic and the sentimental.

Théophile Gautier, one of the authors of *Giselle*, and an uncom-
promising romanticist, was champion of the theory that plastic art had
its place in literature. He was the first to propound the notion of
" art for art's sake ", which is still debated nowadays. It is perhaps
fondness for pure art, for its most plastically definite forms, that led
him to write a Ballet, of all art-forms that which contains the most
plastic element and the most abstract beauty.

" Whatever he writes ", says René Doumic " Théophile Gautier
always takes his standpoint from the point of view of art, giving
us impressions and feelings that are a painter's. He had started
life as a painter... He used to describe himself as a man for whom
the outer world did exist ". We know that another of his works,
le Roman de la Momie, supplied the canvas of a Ballet, *la Fille du
Pharaon*.

In his delightful tale *Romanticism*, Anatole France describes his
principal character thus : " M. Marc Ribert inspired me with the
greatest admiration. His speech, his eyes, his gesture, were the
very expression of his genius and his dreams. I always saw him
surrounded with Sylphs, Gnomes, Imps, Angels, Demons, and
Fairies. How he would recite now a nebulous *lied*, now a fantastic
ballad ! He used to aver that fair is foul, and foul is fair : and I
unhesitatingly believed him. "

It is from that very world of Sylphs, of Nymphs, and of Willis,
from the cloudy fancies of romantic ballads, from the blending of the
beautiful and the repulsive, of reality and romance, that so many
ballets of the 'thirties and 'forties were derived : the *Sylphs, Undine,
The Magic Lake* and *Giselle*. But all those romantic ballets have
long disappeared from the repertoire, together indeed with the artists
who created then : Taglioni, Ellsler, and Grisi. No other dancers
dared to appear in the parts that owed their popularity to those famous

ballerine. And later, Romanticism declined; new schools and new ballets appeared, as I mentioned before, in the wake of new tendencies in literature.

There seemed to be no longer room for the figments and fancies of the Romantic period. The Elves and Sprites receded into the background where the gods and goddesses of Rome and Greece had previously been consigned.

Certainly, *Giselle* would never have been revived in the twen-

DESIGN FOR THE SECOND ACT OF " GISELLE "
BY J. URBAN

tieth century but for Pavlova, whose gifts proved equal to the enterprise of rescuing that work from the depths of oblivion; of inspiring it with new life, and compelling the spectator of to-day to enjoy it, much as he would enjoy an old print found in a curiosity shop. Under the dismal shadow of the weeping willow, *Giselle's* sisters, the Willis, sleep forever, a dream of Romanticism, together with the aerial Sylphid and the mysterious Undine. But *Giselle* herself has come to life again : Pavlova, a new-born fairy, brings new enchantment to the audiences of to-day.

II

The French public of the 'forties read a good deal of the works of the German Romanticists, and especially of Heine.

The first notion of *Giselle* originated in Heine's delightful *De l'Allemagne*.

" My dear Heine " wrote Théophile Gautier " a few weeks ago, glancing through your wonderful book, I found a delightful passage

— as one is bound to do whenever one opens the book at random : the passage in which you mention the Elves in white robes whose hem is always damp, the Nixes who show their milk-white foot through the ceiling of the nuptial chamber, the pale Willis and their fatal waltz, in short, all the marvelous beings that you met with in the Hartz and on the banks of the Ilse, in the mellow mist of a German moonlight. Involuntarily I exclaimed : " What a wonderful ballet that would make ! " And in a fit of enthusiasm I took a nice big sheet of white paper, and in my best hand wrote on it that title : " The Willis, ballet. "

" Then I burst out laughing, and threw the sheet away, thinking that it would be most difficult to express on the stage that wealth of aerial, nocturnal poetry. "

Three days later, the Ballet *Giselle* was written and accepted. In a week Adolphe Adam extemporised the music, Ciceri painted the scenery, imbuing it with all the mystery of the fantastic period. The rehearsals were eagerly pushed forward, and on June 21, 1841, *Giselle* was produced on the stage of the Opera, as radiant, poetical and triumphant an apparition as could be imagined.

His " plastic " conception of art enabled Théophile Gautier fully to realise how suitable for a Ballet Heine's legend was. Carlotta

Grisi (who had recently appeared on the stage of the Opera, taking the place of the older stars Taglioni and Elssler) had become the idol of the public. Gautier himself admired her greatly, and was desirous of writing for her something really wothy of her talent. And in composing *Giselle ou les Willis*, he had a useful cooperator, Saint Georges. Of Adam's music he writes :

" He has never shown more grace, greater tenderness and melancholy. The second act especially is instinct with fantasy most suitable in character : the blue moonbeams glide mysteriously along the silvery notes of the music, and across the waters of the most transparent of lakes ever painted by Ciceri. "

The illustration on page 75 conveys a true impression of the mystical character given to *Giselle* on the stage of the Paris Opéra. It is a faithful reproduction of the original woodcut published in a book now very rare, " les Beautés de l'Opéra ou Chefs-d'œuvre lyriques " (1845).

" M. Coralli (the Ballet-master) " Gautier continues " has shown in the dancing and in the staging that he remains the most juvenile of our choregraphists. "

The parts of *Giselle* and of the young duke were entrusted to Grisi and to Petipa respectively. Théophile Gautier speaks of their performance as follows : " The third act becomes a genuine poem, a choregraphic elegy full of charm and tenderness. Many eyes that were prepared merely to gaze upon *ronds-de-jambe* and *pointes* were unexpectedly dimmed by tears — an occurrence most unusual during a ballet performance. The part is henceforth one that no other dancer will dare attempt : Carlotta's name cannot be severed from *Giselle*. " Gautier spoke the truth, for no other dancer ever took up the part from Grisi's days to the day when Pavlova appeared in it.

III

In the chapter, " Pavlova as a classical dancer ", I have said that the thorough individuality of her gifts, her imponderability, her aerial grace, directed her for good and all towards the mysterious beauties of Romanticism, whose paths she faithfully continued to tread and to extend. She became the faraway princess of a land of dreams, a land haunted by the misty shadows of Sylphs, Mermaids, and Willis, by all the magic fancies and raptures of elegies and ballads. That is why she was attracted by *Giselle*, that choregraphic gem of the romantic period; and why her creation of the part constitutes the perfect revelation of her genius.

" Giselle is a fascinating maiden with deep wistful eyes, with innocent lips that smile beautifully, aerial and graceful... When the dramatic part of the ballet develops, the artist transcends all the hopes that the spectators had placed in her. Not one conventional attitude, not one gesture smacking of artifice : all is life, pure and simple. She floats along the stage, she is in her natural sphere, far from the commonplaces of the *terre à terre*. She is the daughter of

ANNA PAVLOVA
IN " LES SYLPHIDES "
BY VALENTINE-J. HUGO

the breeze, born in the clear imponderable aether of melody. One could not imagine a dance more masterful, more consummately exquisite in every detail, more graceful, more instinct with rhythm and numerosity." Thus did Théophile Gautier write in the good old days when Grisi created the part.

I fell sure that the author of *Giselle*, if in a dream of this world he could behold Pavlova in his Ballet, would not only refrain from erasing one word of his enthusiastic appreciation, but emphasise Pavlova's profound understanding of the style of his period. He would underline the magic, the perfect artistic delicacy and pregnancy of the talent that enabled her to master the very spirit of those times so distant in the background, to reincarnate the pathetic, sweet and simple maiden, and the elegiac aerial Willis. O, the depths of the sadness in the eyes of that wronged maiden, a mere child! The diaphaneity and melancholy of the Willis who, bathed in moonlight, arises out of the tomb! Her childlike, unsophisticated joy, her deep grief, are in turn transmitted from the stage to the audience : and that bond uniting the artist and the onlookers is the supreme achievement of Pavlova's unique, entrancing talent.

When the curtain falls upon her flower-decked grave, the spectator grieves to feel that there ends the wonderful tale; that the enchanted kingdom of the most enchanting of Willis has vanished. But he will treasure in his soul the vision of the almost immateriate girl, a vision that seems made of pallid moonbeams and silvery mists, of the fragrance of flowers, of the floating sounds of melodies as simple and pure as is *Giselle* herself.

Amidst the turmoil and worries of our times, it is blissful indeed to find for a while a refuge in that oasis of clear, pure poetry, the realm of the peerless artist whose privilege it is to carry us so far from the harsh prose of life, to refresh our weary minds with the wonders of her dancing; a boon of which we carry away a grateful memory. All who have seen Pavlova as *Giselle* express their admiration for her acting and dancing in that old masterpiece, that delightful blend of impassioned drama and poetic choregraphy.

Although of comparatively small proportions, *Giselle* is a ballet that remains beyond the power of any dancer whose gifts are purely technical. It is seldom that a talent for mimic action goes with a talent for dancing, let alone the capacity for holding the stage, the expressiveness of the face and body, and the capacity for true style. Alone a complete, most comprehensive talent, a gift for communicating emotion and inspiring the spectators with genuine belief in the beauties of the dramatic action displayed before them will enable an artist to succeed in the little part of *Giselle*. And that is the reason why *Giselle* is so seldom revived.   The part was attempted at Petrograd in 1841 by Andréïanova, who later danced at Paris and ended her days there.   Afterwards, Lucille Grahn made a similar attempt, without success.   Even greater was Grimaldi's failure at a later date.   Then *Giselle* sank into oblivion, until revived by Pavlova. Of Pavlova can be said, without exaggeration, what the delighted poets of the 'thirties used to say of Taglioni, their idol : " She is a nymph, a shadow, an angel, a sylph; she is a passing breeze, a soul floating above a tomb... all remained silent in order to *hear* her dancing, as tuneful as a *song*. "

IV

Whoever has seen Pavlova as Giselle will always remember the languid, melancholy expression of her features — a vision, as in a dream, of the whole character of a bygone time.

In the first act, while she dances joyfully with her youthful sweetheart, she already conveys a vague, yet harping impression of fatality.   An atmosphere of sadness surrounds her : the bare shadow of a cloud approaching from afar, and reflected amid the merry ripples

on the surface of the lake. When her dream of love collapses, with the sudden shock, tragedy breaks into the peaceful idyll. And with the scene of her madness, — that most conventional and most hackneyed episode — the call for unusual resourcefulnesss and sense of proportion becomes greater than ever : otherwise the scene would be unpleasant, and fail to carry conviction. If an interpreter falls short in the matter of power, subtlety and style, she can easily turn this scene into a repulsive and needless episode, a mere stage-effect of the most meretricious kind. From the very outset, Pavlova's interpretation conveys the impression that Giselle is an ephemeral creature, not intended to live amid her fellow men in their commonplace surroundings. Only for a fleeting instant has she assumed a corporeal shape, in the little village beyond the Rhine. She hails from another world, bringing with her a glimpse of its mysteries, of the mists and shadows where unembodied beings pass in noiseless pageant, floating in the moonlight, silently dancing, fascinating the dreamers and leading them to their doom.

Pavlova's smile, half joyful, half sad, her eyes full of love and secret anguish, her dreamy pauses, her nimble and supple motions, all helps to reveal that strange, mysterious world, from which she has but come, and to which she will so soon return.

Pavlova's composition of her part shows that she has concen-

trated, as in a trance, upon her main conception of it. Therefore, every detail, to the most minute, cooperates in its one general effect, tends with forceful directness — the apparent result of unconscious inspiration — towards an intuitive resurrection of the true Giselle.

And Pavlova's innermost idiosyncrasies, which seem to have been created and combined precisely in view of *Giselle,* make that resurrection most convincing. They afford her endless possibilities for her impersonation. Her physical beauty is not, like that of a statue, immutable and moveless, but as supple and versatile as her conception of her art is. It varies in accordance with her moods and, as one critic has aptly remarked, " she is in absolute command of her own beauty, which is lit up with every flame that arises from her soul, to burn bright with every one of her movements, with every flash of her inspiration ".

The secret of her wonderful achievement lies in the perfectly harmonious cooperation of all that she does; in the wonderful equivalence of her intentions and her deeds, and in the fusion of every element into one beautifully balanced whole, which constitutes artistic finality. Should one attempt to analyse the methods through which Pavlova manages to convey so rare and telling an artistic impression, one is deeply surprised to discover how extremely simple they are. Let one but remember Giselle's madness, that scene so conventional, and to which so very few bars of the score are devoted. Giselle, struck down by the catastrophe, gradually recovers consciousness; and with the return of consciousness come fragmentary recollections of past happiness. The orchestra plays the tune to which she danced in the days her bliss, and suddenly her recollection becomes clear. Some force seems to compel her to remember the steps of that dance, and those steps she performs, joyless, lifeless, sadly and heavily, as if in the meantime she was hearing some distant call seeing some distant vision...

M. Levinson, the critic, has most aptly characterised that moment in the following words : " With greater power than could have been achieved throught the accurate reproduction of the gestures of actual lunacy, with bent back and a fixed stare, Pavlova expresses the tragical wreckage of her innocent soul in the deformation of the very dance-rhythm, in her anguished, faltering, broken dancing "; the very thing that Théophile Gautier described as " a few straggling steps, a kind of choregraphic agony ".

Oscar Bie, who has written in German a book on Pavlova, says that " her rendering of the madness in *Giselle* is one of the greatest achievements, in the matter of dramatic art, ever arrived at through the medium of dancing. That scene, although consisting but of dumb show, is so strong in its appeal, that it enables us to understand the enthusiasm of the French of olden times, who would often prefer the arresting impression produced by a well-performed pantomime to the direct reality of the spoken drama. Both elements are associated in her : she acts the dancing, and dances the acting ; she informs the old art with the spirit of to-day's life, and brings naturalism under the sway of a perfectly regulated technique. I am thinking, above all, of her impersonation of Giselle in that ballet built so closely upon the lines of the *Opéra-Comique*, holding the balance even between pantomime and technical steps. She speaks not : but her person embodies certain lines that are the music of motion, the melody of the hands, the harmony of the body, which all create in us the vision of a great tragic actress. She appears : and within a few instants so great a wealth and turmoil of rhythms arise, that we can but admire and wonder, realising the treasures of silent music and plastic beauty which lie concealed in her. "

No less simple are the devices, purely choregraphic and technical, that she uses in the second act, when Giselle has become a Willis. In the fragrant vernal night, the moonbeams fall upon her grave. She arises, surrounded with shadow and mystery. In the

murky underground realm of Death, the peasant girl has been transformed into a winged wraith. Rejoicing to see the world again, she floats across the air, now swinging upon a branch, now hiding behind the foliage, full of sheer happiness, until the return of dawn calls her back to the tomb. Then she bids a grave and sad farewell to her grief-stricken lover, and dies again, vanishing among the flowers. Tenderly, the beautiful shrubs and roses bend over her, as if to murmur in her ear some secret message, and hide her from all dwellers upon earth. It is all as simple as life, as beautiful as a fairy tale; it is a most lovely poem without words. And no words could express the beauty of Pavlova's dancing, which compels the spectators to believe in the reality of the dream, to take their part with her in the progress of the drama.

And her dances, I repeat it, are very simple, devoid of far-fetched and obtrusive *tours de force :* Pavlova's instinct warned her that all such effects would be out of keeping. But when in her famous *pas de deux* she springs up in the air, supported by her partner, the leap is so powerful, so aerial, that she seems to take possession, all of a sudden, of the infinity of space. And after one moment of silent wonder and suspense, her feat is greeted with long and thunderous applause. Another wonderful effect is when Pavlova, on tiptoe, crosses the stage diagonally, advancing towards the foreground. Those " pointes " constitute no rare trick, and are not particularly difficult perhaps. There is no dancer of the technical school who does not attempt the like. But what Pavlova does, or rather, the way in which she does it, remains unique. And again the delighted audience expresses its rapture by endless ovations. While Pavlova performs that course, she is actually a shadow; she crosses the floor without creating the least vibration, she barely touches the ground. Her body remains moveless; the eye perceives no oscillation, no inclination, not even the tremble of a muscle. One is really facing a ghost, one feels hallucinated. One sees, and does not trust one's eyes; one is carried into the very heart of legend and romance. One feels that after all, those incorporeal Willis may have existed of yore. After having seen Pavlova as Giselle, the well known dramatic critic J. Belaief described her as " an arrow, infinitely light and slender; the last echo of a lovely and distant past. She flies, she radiates, she playfully twinkles in the aether of the stage. There is but one Pavlova, a scintillating thing of beauty, a spirit, a beam of light. As Giselle, she is the incarnation of an old masterpiece of engraving, suddenly come to life. She appears, spreads her veils, and enters the kingdom of pure dance. She is a live arabesque, her dancing is that of a mere spirit. The mischievous little head, the little body, the tiny feet that carry her into the air — all that is a delightful image sprung up from our grandmothers' times ".

Pavlova was indeed intended by nature for the romantic ballet, for the evocation of the kingdom of dreams, that kingdom so attractive to every lover of pure art, beloved by Voltaire, Rousseau and Pushkin, where inviolate seas bathe undiscovered shores, and where there is no utilitarian life, but only the emotions of pure rhythm, of pure beauty and of poetry at its best.

Of that kingdom Pavlova is the Queen Mab,
> " In shape no bigger than an agate stone
> On the forefinger of an alderman "

who dispenses dreams and fancies weird or graceful, joyous or sad, but always instinct with beauty, felicitous, and soul-stirring.

And it is because of those essential qualities of her art that her appearance in that pristine, old-fashioned, forgotten *Giselle* constitues a memorable event. It is she who, with the convincing power of genius, gave the signal for that reversion to the older forms of the art of dancing which is to-day universal.

By way of conclusion we shall quote the following curious

excerpts from a long letter which Théophile Gautier, the librettist of *Giselle,* wrote to Heine, to whom he was indebted for the legend of the Willis, after the performance of the Ballet.   It is quite surprising to learn from this letter that in Théophile Gautier's original scheme, the first act was entirely different from what it became in the final version.

Théophile Gautier wrote :

" Being entirely ignorant of all that concerns theatrical combinations and of the requirements of the stage, I had thought at first that a dramatisation of Victor Hugo's delightful *Orientale* would suffice for the first act.   One would have seen a beautiful ballroom in the palace of a prince, with eve-

rything ready for the festivity : chandeliers alight, flowers in all the vases, refreshments on the dressers ; but as yet no sign of the guests. The Willis would have made a brief appearance, attracted by the prospect of dancing in the brilliant surroundings of the hall, and also by the hope of finding some new recruit for their company.   The Queen of the Willis would have touched the flooring with her magic wand, in order to infect all the dancers with an ardent desire for waltzes and mazurkas and farandolas. The arrival of the guests would have caused the Wilis to vanish like so many shadows. Giselle, after having danced the whole night, would have fallen a victim to the cold of the morning, and the Queen of the Willis, would have come to placed her ice-cold hand upon the unfortunate maiden's heart. But we should have been deprived of the admirably performed scene with which the first act ends; and the second act would have lost part of the element of surprise to which it owes some of its effectiveness ".

Fortunately indeed for *Giselle,* this peculiar notion was not carried out. The poet was led by his sound understanding of the requirements of romanticism to invent another plot, whose tragical ending enabled the two great impersonators of the title-part, Grisi and Pavlova, to stamp that part with their respective individualities.

At the end of his letter, Théophile Gautier pays tribute to the composer of the music in terms of warm admiration — but in terms which it is hard to read without a feeling of surprise, because he describes that pleasant, but light music as instinct with science : " Adolphe Adam's music teems with motives and orchestral effects. The score even contains, for the special benefit of those who love recondite music, an admirably written fugue. The second act felicitously solves the musical problem of combining fancy with grace, and is replete with tuneful melodies. Carlotta was recalled amid thunderous applause from the whole audience ".

The same remark applies to Pavlova. Indeed, we have been unable to keep tally of the calls which testified to the enthusiasm of all those who saw her wonderful rendering of the part in Paris.

PAVLOVA'S OTHER CREATIONS

OUNTLESS were Pavlova's creations after *Giselle*. The first place may be given to *The Swan's Death*.

The origin of that theme of solo dancing is simple enough. Once upon a time, Saint-Saëns published, under the collective title *Le Carnaval des Animaux* a set of pieces, one of which bore the name *La Mort du Cygne*. Fokine conceived the idea of turning that little piece (which is written for harp) to choregraphic purposes, and Pavlova that of dancing it. It was in London that Saint-Saëns saw for the first time Pavlova's interpretation of his *Cygne*. After the show he went behind the scenes, and expressed his admiration in the warmest terms.

" Candidly " he said, " I feared desecration for my music. But what I have seen is an artistic whole, in which music and dancing associate in perfect harmony ".

There can be no doubt that of the three elements that cooperate to the general effect — music, choregraphy and execution — the third, here, is by far the most important. As I have found myself compelled to repeat more than once, it is impossible to subject Pavlova's art to matter-of-fact analysis. To the soft lullaby of the harp, alone, a beautiful bird appears, bathed in pallid moonrays. A mute appeal in her eye, a waving of her hands, like trembling wings, a few " pointes ", and the perfect harmony and grace of every curve and movement. Nothing more. And many a dancer after Pavlova has staked on that " winning number. " One did tolerably well, another not so well, a third quite well. But what they did remained an ordinary solo turn, nothing more. What Pavlova does makes it a wonderful masterpiece of plastical art. One may ask, why so great a difference? The reply is, that in those short chore-graphic poems, ballads or elegies, in those plastical songs, the dra-matisation of dancing plays an all-important part : and the power adequately to dramatise dancing is one of Pavlova's chief assets. Danced by her, the *Swan's Death* is not a mere " variation " unim-peachably performed, nor a mere realistic imitation of the wounded bird : it is the mystic elegy of a fated ending, translated into the soulful poetry of dramatised dance.

The late critic Belaief wrote: " There is something touching and seductive about her art ; something frail and wistful, which actually suggests the legend of the swan. I see in her the enchanted princess of fairy tales, transformed into a snow-white swan, grieving, strug-gling, flapping her beautiful wings. At the mysterious moment of her stage-reincarnation, she flies about, shyly looks round... Among her companions she stands alone, for royal blood flows in her veins, and they are not her equals. In her steps and leaps, the very beauty and sadness of the swan find their true expression. "

Louis Laloy, the eminent French musical critic, speaks no less highly her praises : " Ten years ago I saw for the first time that queen — or, I would say, that angel — of dance perform that piece at a London music-hall... The impression produced was immediate and powerful : from the stalls to the upper galleries, the audience, until then noisy, subsided into absolute silence until it burst out into cheers and applause. So great is the prestige of art! Nowadays, I find the *Swan's Death* even more wonderful, because I am able better to perceive every detail ; and that again is the distinctive mark of a masterpiece — far from growing surfeited of it, one is constantly discovering in it fresh beauties.

" Remaining for long periods on tiptoe, she translated into lithe

Photo Hoppé.

PAVLOVA
IN THE " BUTTERFLY "

undulations of the arms and slight quivers of the body, the bird's silent progress across the water, the shivering of the plumage ; then suddenly, yet without heaviness, dropping to the ground, the plunge, the reappearance on the surface, the anxiety, the languishing; further, the collapse ending into that last wonderful gesture of pudicity in death, the hiding of the head under an arm like to a wing. So true is each movement, that the little wings added to the tunic appear superfluous. It is dancing only, and its connotations, that here translate the subject; it was the dancing, not the costume, that occupied our minds. "

Maurice Denis quotes a remarkable saying of Puvis de Chavannes : " corresponding to any clear idea, there exists a plastical idea that translates it. " From that point of view, it is quite clear that the symbolism of Pavlova's movements and steps and attitudes in things such as *The Swan's Death* and many other creations of hers is nothing but the expression, in plastic form, of the emotions which the subject calls forth in her soul.

In other words, expression on the stage, generally speaking, is not a thing essentially dependent upon realistic attempts. On the contrary : in all types of art, the more the creative artist refrains from slavishly copying nature, the more faithful and striking the rendering, the interpretation of nature, which he will give us, illuminated and coloured by the rays of the light which his own mind casts upon it; and the richer in features which will reveal unto us nature not only in its externals, but in its very essence. And that is why we so often see that the more abstract a picture the great artists give us, the more convincing and live that picture is.

Pavlova's creations afford more than one case in point. They include many instances of pure nature-painting, vivid interpretations of life as seen in nature and translated into art forms, art forms never actually realistic, yet full of truth at its purest and best : such are her Swan, her Butterfly, her Dragon-Fly, and even that delightful incarnation of flower-life, her Californian Poppy. One and all are plastic expressions of what her soul and mind have actually experienced, not conventional or realistic imitations. And that is why they are great.

I should not like to lay myself open to the slightest suspicion of partiality or one-sidedness : yet it is impossible not to say practically the same thing of every creation of Pavlova when considering them singly. Therefore, I shall now proceed to quote the opinions expressed by French critics of various tendencies, which more than confirm what I have written above.

Héliog.Schützenberger

ANNA PAVLOVA
Portrait par Schuster-Woldan

WATER-COLOUR DRAWING FOR CLEOPATRA'S COSTUME
BY LÉON BAKST

PAVLOVA AND VOLININ
IN THE " BACCHANAL "

Pavlova's reapparance in Paris after a protracted absence was hailed as a revelation.

In the *Figaro*, Régis Gignoux wrote: " We had forgotten that there could be such a concourse of the Tout-Paris, of that great family so vast that cousins and nephews have to be introduced to one another. But at last we have seen them all assembled... not all, alas! For many were missing, whose seats were occupied by new-comers, by people who had never yet seen Pavlova. Those new-comers gloated on Pavlova intently; their looks betokened admiration and wonder, but wonder mixed with astonishment. It seemed as though they suspected a trick of some kind, some sort of magic or deception. That wonderful *vol plané* across the stage, those aerial leaps, did the dancer really achieve them without the help of a steel wire and pulley?

" Look again, you neophytes. And you will realise that this artist has come to replace the image destroyed by the Barbarians, to reinstate the cult of dancing. Yon dying swan is the propitiatory victim; in it you see Pavlova, the new Iphigenia, atoning for your fox-trots, tangos and jazz-bands.

" After the classical beauty of the Ballet " The Snowflakes " came *Les Préludes*, a thing of sweetness, of serene coolness and calm. Then that wonder, *The Dying Swan*. How can Pavlova be so loftily elegiac in a thing so perilously near to ineptitude? Alone, her physical gifts would have been impotent : the saving grace of her emotion, of her genuine faith, was needed. And the same may be said of the impassioned, glowing *Danse Syrienne* with which the spectacle ended ".

No less enthusiastic is G. de Pavlowsky, who writes in *Le Journal* : " To elicit tears by resorting to simulacra of actual life is nothing. But to shake the soul to its utmost depths, making it vibrate in perfect attunement with the principle of Beauty which lurks in those depths, is a privilege almost divine. At moments such as these, all modes of expression cease to exist as things apart, all arts converge, nothing remains but pure emotion, abstract enough to constitute an absolute, apart from the shifting illusions of life's spectacles.

" How did it happen that for a few seconds, when the Russian dancers reappeared before our eyes, we felt again that powerful inner joy? To attempt to explain the fact would be bootless, for that joy transcends all modes of expression. We must content ourselves with describing the various things to which we owed it.

" After a display of that virtuosity which makes Pavlova's the world's greatest classical dancer, it was chiefly the very instant of the Swan's death. How beautiful artistic, how full of style is Pavlova's rendering of the wounded bird's terror, agony, resignation, and gradual collapse! All that indeed is art of a very lofty kind. But the final stage is something even more wonderful: the tragic sweetness of that death eclipses all the grace that was life's. "

Photo Van Riel.

PAVLOVA
IN " THE SWAN'S DEATH "

In *L'Avenir,* Nozière, the famous critic and playwright, expresses the following opinion :

" Pavlova's gestures are instinct with harmony ; there is intelligence in her arms. Her interpretation of the Swan' Death, to the music by Saint-Saëns, betokens a most delicate sensitiveness. Three times the audience started cheering her while she was performing that short dance. For the sake of those few minutes only, the public would willingly come to the Théâtre des Champs-Elysées. It is something soft and tremulous and aerial. We see the melancholy of the wounded being, unwilling to die, a last appeal to life, light, and blue sky ; we see attitudes that fully recall the majestic aspect of the noble bird — a majesty whose voluptuous character was acknowledged by the artists of old Greece. And Pavlova's triumph is fully deserved ".

Andrei Levensohn, the Russian critic, writes : " Among Pavlova's minor creations, one, *The Swan's Death,* is a thing never to be for-

PAVLOVA AND MORDKIN
IN " THE RUSSIAN DANCE "

gotten.   Posterity will bestow on it the same halo of legend as upon *Giselle* and *The Dancing Girl*.

   " Pavlova, the Swan, appears, her arms folded, and on tip-toe circles dreamily and slowly round the stage.   Carried by slow, even, gliding motions of her hands, she gradually reaches the background, seems to strive towards the horizon, ready to fly away.   For a long while she stands tensely poised, as though gazing upon the realms of space. And gradually she relaxes, she sinks, her arms faintly waving as under the impulse of pain; hurried, uneven steps bring her towards the foot-lights, her legs quivering like the strings of a harp. One beautiful movement then brings her right foot forwards, while she sinks on her left knee — and with that movement, unspeakably tense and telling, she dies.

" Here again, she resorts to the disintegration of rhythms to express pain and distress, as she did in the first act of *Giselle*.

" With her, the method leads to invaluable results so far as dramatic expression is concerned. Out of the melancholy suggestion embodied in Saint-Saën's tone-picture, out of the clear, simple symbols supplied by Fokin's choregraphy, the dancer has evolved that wonderful " White Death ", the death of the aerial being struggling against its earthly bonds. It is a most splendid achievement ".

In *The Swan's Death*, Pavlova gives us the subtlest, most delicate half-tones and shades, the most touching emotions, the most refined and beautiful things in the way of attitudes, of movements, of choregraphic design and colouring. She also achieves genuine pathos. Should we consider her steps from the point of view of technical analysis, we should see that she conveys the impression of originality by the very simplest means — one might say, the most elementary.

It is, however, because whatever she does is instinct with the glow of her impassioned sense of truth and beauty, is the result of eager, earnest concentration, translated into the subtlest plastic symbols. Within the same cycle of her interpretations, those that refer to animal life, the next two we have to consider are *The Butterfly* and the *Dragon-Fly*.

Both those miniature masterpieces afford her occasion to give us the very antithesis of *The Swan's Death* : that is, pictures of sheer joy, of overflowing spirits, of beings dancing without a care amidst the surroundings of happy, sun-clad landscapes.

There again, Pavlova has discovered the true colours, the true plastic modes of expression. Her buoyant, blithesome *Dragon-Fly*, her elated, light-hearted *Butterfly*, are tiny, yet splendid gems of poetic dancing, beautiful little lyrics without words.

I can remember a certain evening at Moscow when the audience was roused to such a pitch of enthusiasm by the charm and beauty of Pavlova's *Butterfly*, that the artist had to repeat the dance three times. It is impossible to pay too high a tribute to so delightful an expression of the joy of life, of sunny spring-time, of warm fragrant breezes. Those " little tales from the book of nature " contain something greather than dancing : something that we realise and appreciate without the help of analytical comment, of which we are instinctively and directly conscious, and which our mind conceives forthwith as Beauty of the rarest and most precious kind. There is no need scientifically to determine the beauty of her dancing. Indeed, we feel it before we have time to analyse or comprehend. Besides, does one ever " understand " beauty?

From the point of view of choregraphic technique, all those three little pictures, *The Swan's Death, The Butterfly* and *The Dragon-Fly* are nothing more intricate than studies in toe-dancing, in " pointes ", a thing that all trained classical dancers are capable of performing : but Pavlova transforms those mere studies into pearls of price, pearls which owe their warm, delicate lustre to the flame of the artist's inspiration — a flame whose light pervades her dancing, gives life to each step and pose. Pavlova never contents herself with the mere literalities of technical rules.

Her extreme virtuosity, her brilliant technique, are not things to be acquired merely through long years of sedulous labour and practice, by dint of exercises and industry. In her dancing, all complications of detail resolve themselves into the simplicity of the whole. Even the most elementary things become substantial, concentrated, eloquent. But it is when her head droops in sadness, when her eyes express the mute hopeless appeal, when in a last shudder she dies in the soft moonlight of the summer night, that we realise the power of her art to the full : the very coldness of death lurks in that swan-song. When, on the contrary, her hands flutter like the butterfly's wings, it seems as though she was bringing in her wake all the sweet perfumes and golden rays of spring. With the swift vibrations of the Dragon-Fly's gauzy wings come all the glow and warmth of summer, of sunshine bathing green swards and happy fields. And there is another picture of life, *The Little Fish*, which strikingly translates the easy, smooth vibrations and curves amidst the clear undulating waves. All those tales of nature's wonders are narrated on the stage in a way which carries conviction as well as surpassing delight.

They are tales of no particular date, from no particular country : tales as old, as universal as life ; and perhaps even more beautiful than life, because they are the very essence, the concentrated sap of life transmuted into perfect art. In the form which Pavlova gives them,

Photo Van Riel.

PAVLOVA
IN THE " BACCHANAL "

they are more powerful than they could be in words : for words soon become threadbare, and even sooner puerile. Tutchef, the Russian poet, certainly realised the deficiencies of words when he wrote that " every idea, when expressed in words, becomes a falsehood ". Words cannot translate moods nor feelings. But Pavlova's silent interpretations, instinct with the very life of nature, carry the spectators away from the dark, closed auditorium into the magic realms of fairy-tale : she communicates her own moods so convincingly, that whoever sees her carries away within his soul a spark from the fire which burns in her and inspires her.

Let us now cease to consider the delightful creations for which she derived her inspiration from the pure clear founts of nature, and turn to her interpretation of human emotions: we will see that she is as profound as psychologist as she is an observer of bird, animal, and insect life. Indeed it is difficult to decide which of those two spheres is the one in which she displays to the fullest her sense of colour and her power for expression. And in the latter sphere, we see her interpreting with equal depth of understanding and convincing genuineness the East and the West, the dances of Syria or Egypt and those of Europe, in every case creating around herself the true atmosphere, and paying attention, with valuable artistic results, to every historical and ethnographical point. But let us start with a few words upon the subject of her Oriental dances.

The Syrian Dance, to music by Saint-Saëns (which has been mentioned in a previous chapter) is as beautiful as the choicest miniatures of old Persia. In it she indulges in a wonderful display of choregraphic pyrotechnics, flaming spirals, impassionned attitudes, wonderful combinations of curves and arabesques. Her dancing is instinct with the very soul of the East.

Upon the stage a few Eastern merchants, who seem to have walked straight out of the *Arabian Nights,* are trying to tempt a girl, as lithe and slender as a young palm-tree, by the display of their wares: precious stones, rare fruit, mirrors of gold and silver, gorgeous many-hued fabrics. She pounces eagerly upon all those treasures. But as she beholds her reflection in a mirror, her woman's instinct prompts her to select a filmy, variegated silk. And then begins a set of dances wonderful beyond description. Quick breathless tempi; the utmost fantasy in movements and attitudes ; the incredible suppleness of her limbs and body, the versatility and power of expression of her face and hands and feet — all contributes to the extraordinary beauty of that little masterpiece of Orientalism.

That dance has inspired several painters and sculptors, among whom the Belgian, Stevens, who has painted a superb portrait of Pavlova in that part.

With the *Syrian Dance* Pavlova makes us fall in love with the East in its warmth and glamour, the East of which she calls up a delicate and in a way a humoristic vision. In the *Bacchanal,* to music by Glazunof, the picture she gives of Greek antiquity is one of intense glow and feverish passion. Strewing flowers right and left, the Bacchant is dancing along the edge of a wood. The blossoms are scattered to the wind, her long curls dance about her soulders, the ceaselessly shifting folds of the white tunic reveal the shapely limbs and body. She dances like a flame, she is something bewildering and dazzling. She resurrects for us the very soul and spirit behind the Orgiastic rites, the very secret of that " mystical intoxications " of the old choregraphy. Here is, indeed, the elemental Dionysios, pictured in an artistic creation so spontaneous, so obviously the outcome of untramelled, genuine, far-seeing inspiration, that we see nothing of Pavlova's studious investigations of sources and documents, of her researches in libraries and museums, of her studies of statuary and painted vases : for all the results of her work are embodied into that wonderful elemental thing, her dancing.

Let us consider that other instance of Bacchanalian dancing, Wagner's *Venusberg*, in Isadora Duncan's interpretation. How very lifeless, meaningless, and small it appears in comparison with the lambent flame of Pavlova's *Bacchanal!* For what Pavlova gives us is not the purely scholarly beauty of a reconstitution, by an erudite dancer, of what the friezes which can be seen in museums teach us; it is the live beauty of victorious creation, of inspiration freely asserted, and subject to no laws but those of the creative artist's own feelings and inner sense of rhythm and proportions.

The *Oriental Dance* is another creation instinct with the spirit of the East. But our object is not to enumerate one by one the priceless gems which she has extracted from the inexhaustible mine towards which the Eastern Muse has led her steps. And we must now turn our attention to other aspects of her activities.

Suddenly to pass, in Pavlova's wake, from the glowing aspects of Eastern fantasy to the eerie dreaminess and misty settings of Northern romance is an extraordinary experience.

In that latter order, nothing is more typical than " The Falling Leaves ", a scene for which Pavlova found inspiration in music by Chopin, that peerless exponent of musical romanticism. It is a little picture instinct with the melancholy poetry of autumn, composed by Pavlova herself (who has revealed herself as a first class ballet-master); the elegy of late grey days, of clouds and mists and colder wind — a thing so full of feeling, so introspective and genuine in its picturesqueness and poetry, that it ranks among the most precious masterpieces of lyric choregraphy.

In " The Falling Leaves ", we see a poet in love with a beautiful chrysanthemum which is growing in the favourite corner of his flower-garden. A cold autumn wind has bruised the lovely blossom, which now stands fading. The poet, overcome with grief, remains unmoved when his fiancée appears and presents him with another chrysanthemum. At eventide, the winds rises, leaves begin to fall, and the drooping flower which the poet is vainly striving to keep alive dies. Sadly the poet leaves the garden with his fiancée. One might describe the scene as a conflict between the poetry of life and its prose, between ideal, spiritual love and matter-of-fact love. It is a brief, but thorough synthesis of feelings and emotions, beautifully conceived and expressed in the idiom of choregraphy. It contains no "libretto-literature", it consists wholly of mood-pictures and purely choregraphic or mimic modes of expression. And the impression it creates upon audiences is correspondingly immediate and deep.

In the part of the chrysanthemum, Pavlova rises to so high an artistic level, is so genuinely impressive and so simple in all she does, that the sweet dream of autumn created by her fancy and expressed in her dancing remains in the spectators' mind long after the curtain has fallen. The corps-de-ballet, impersonating the leaves driven by the wind, performs most graceful and suitable evolutions, and falls into strikingly beautiful groups ; the lovely setting, all in autumnal yellows and russet, in conjunction with the costumes of similar hues, is in itself a delight, and altogether in keeping with the spirit of Pavlova's conception and of Chopin's pensive, elegiac music.

Another delightful revery belonging to the same order of pictures of romantic fantasy is the *Chopiniana,* in which Pavlova appears clad in a long dancing skirt after the fashion of 1830, and wearing a wreath upon the smooth waves of her dark hair. Swathed in moonlight she comes forth, and in the magic language of her limbs and head and torso proceeds to recite mystic, dreamy poems without words, conveying a most wonderful impression of eloquence and of style — a creation second to none in her repertory or any other.

Then comes *The Night,* to Rubinstein's famous song, which in her interpretation acquires novel interest and increased significance. In the atmosphere of the sweet, fragrant, rapturous night described by the poet, a night of elusive dreams, of fairy-like visions, of glowing hopes and melancholy musings, she revives for us the times of romanticism in all their most typical aspects.

We see her emerge from the mist on tiptoe, barely touching the ground, her hands full of flowers. Lithe, fragile, graceful, she yields to the call of love that fills the air, sweet, alluring, imperative. We feel that the whole being of that slender youthful maiden before us is intent upon responding to the call. And all of a sudden, the call finds an echo in her very self; she arises, glowing, inspired; and her dancing expresses the soul-stirring emotions by which she is carried away.

The Valse-Caprice, to another famous piece of music by Rubinstein, help us to realise with fresh delight the extent of Pavlova's extraordinary versatility. In that charming little scene, she shows us a young coquette for whom life is one continues revel, one long feast of flowers and songs and dances and flirtations and kisses. Happiness and grace, slyness and fanciful sweetness, are wonderfully blended in that delightful miniature.

In *Noël,* to the piece entitled *December* from Tchaïkovsky's set *The Twelve Months,* Pavlova gives us a *tableau-de-genre* which faithfully translates in its romantic aspects the spirit of the forties. There her part is that of a frivolous society girl, who likes to tease her suitors and lead them a hard life, reserving her favours for him whom her heart has elected. That very image of romantic flirtation recalls to mind a water-colour, of the most transparent quality and tone, drawn with utmost style and instinct with true feeling. It is full of life and grace in its conventional garb.

The Russian critic G. Zigfrid writes :

" What magic is it that enables Pavlova to achieve such marvellous results? Does the question really matter? Specialists may indulge in various sapient discourses, which prove nothing and are, when applied to Pavlova, so many empty words. The important point is that her art fascinates the mind and holds us entranced, that with her, form and substance are merged into one harmonious whole; and that however complex the elements which it may comprise, they one and all have their foundation in pure poetry. "

In historical and ethnographical dances, the greatest difficulty for the artists consists in mastering the spirit of various lands and periods, the spirit of national styles. I have already mentioned that such a result is not achieved merely through means so easily accessible as make-up and costume. To fathom the problem, to solve it by penetrating the very spirit of a race, or a time, is the privilege of inborn capacity and inspiration. I am not referring in particular to *Russian Dances*, dances in which Pavlova expresses so fully the true Russian *mollesse* with its occasional outbursts of fiery, but restrained passion. She is Russian; and therefore, it is only natural that her artistic temperament should lead her perfectly to comprehend and to express in full, down to the utmost detail, all that pertains to Russian folk-dancing. But of Spanish dances she is likewise one of the most original interpreters the world has ever seen. The well-controlled, yet fierce fire of her nature enables her to gives, in the whirlwind of her convolutions and *positions cambrées*, a marvellously true picture of Spain.

Another wonderful instance of her versatility and genius for discrimination is afforded by the *Mexican Dances*, in which she appeared in Paris. One can but wonder how she manages so fully to master the secret of the most remotely exotic styles. That new creation, full of colour and replete with originality, was one of her greatest successes, a success which however could hardly compare with the uninterrupted series of triumphs which the same dances won for her in Mexico. If indeed, as I have heard from eye-witnesses, the Mexicans could be moved to such depth of enthusiasm by the foreigner who had dared come to dance their own national dances in the heart of their own country, does not the fact prove that here again, Pavlova has actually achieved the prodigy of reincarnation, and proved so true to her new personality that the Mexicans, after a first impression of bewilderment, were moved to the utmost pitch of delight?

In historical dances such as the *Gavotte Pavlova*, the *Rondino* to music by Beethoven in Kreisler's arrangement, and in Marinucci's *Menuet dans le style ancien*, an artist such as she is can but find it quite an easy matter to convey in its fulness the impression of styles and periods which she has completely mastered. Among those various minor creations of hers, the one which has enjoyed the greatest and most wide-spread success is undoubtledly the Gavotte. And most deservedly : for it is an instance of rare perfection and distinction, a subtle and restrained picture of aristocratic refinement and chaste classicism, in every respect true to style and enjoyable.

Pavlova's sense of dramatic expression, and the forcible quality of her achievements in that order of dancing, have already been mentioned. It is impossible not to retain a most vivid remembrance of her pathetic, impressive rendering of *The Swan's Death*, of the wonderfully moving tragedy of *Giselle*. And to the list should be added an abridged version of the big ballet *Esmeralda*, which is included in her repertory under the title *Amarilla*. It is, like *Giselle*, a choreographic drama, a human tragedy interpreted in pantomime and dancing. But it is terser than *Giselle*, and calls for more thorough concentration. The interpreter is called upon to express the whole

ANNA PAVLOVA
Poster for the Russian Ballet season
by V. Sérof

range of passions and emotions originating in the bitter disenchant-
ment of unrequited love : she must show that she is compelling
herself to dance in the presence of the man who has broken his
plight to her, and while torn with the jealousy inspired by the
presence of his fiancée; at times she must express the birth of new
hopes, then the pain caused by his indifference and heartlessness,
and lastly, the crushing of all her hopes and desires, the ultimate
despair. If it be remembered that all those things have to happen
within a space of time barely exceeding fifteen minutes, and that the
artist must take hold of her public by her ardour and versatility under
all those different aspects within that short time, then we realise how
extraordinary her achievement is in *Amarilla*. This Ballet consists
of a set of episodes, each distinct, yet all bound together by virtue
of the general unity of tone and mood. It is like a bunch of rays
concentrated through a lens, and converging upon one focus in a
wonderful glow of flame. The versatility of dramatic feeling, the
intensity of expression that characterise her dancing are supreme : yet
the means employed remain as simple as ever. Consider for instance,
her *pizziccato* on tiptoe, the arms slackly drooping, as though bereft
of vitality and no longer controlled by the will, the anxious movements of the head, the sad wan smile, the eyes now weary, now
inflamed with hatred and jealousy, the flexions of the whole body
suddenly betraying the inner torment. Taken singly, each of those
effects, each of those expressions is derived straight from nature in
simplest, most straightforward wise. Coordinated as they are by
Pavlova, they produce an impression of perfect beauty, of supreme
power, they become a perfect work of art.

A few words remain to be said about another order of Pavlova's
activities. In the chapter " Pavlova as a classical dancer ", I attempted to show that if Pavlova's position as a dancer and place in the
history of the choregraphic art are so exceptional, it is because with
her, the classical tradition of dancing serves as a foundation for all
stage dancing, whichever its spirit and kind. We considered in
turn, and in all their surprising diversity, the various things comprised in her extensive repertory : and we realised that in the matter
of classical dancing, her contributions stood supreme, but at the
same time that her versatility was boundless, and that her individuality never failed strongly to assert itself. We owe her masterpieces
in drama; folk-dancing, historic, romantic, ethnographic dancing,
ancient or modern, Eastern or Western, have become dearer to us
because of her. An artist so sensitive, so clear-sighted, so keen in

her quest for knowledge of, and power in, all that concerns her art, was bound to take an active interest in the contemporary evolution of the Ballet and of dancing. The progress and transformation taking place under her eyes she always watched eagerly and sympathetically. But, of course, in her capacity as an artist who had thoroughly found herself and knew exactly what she wanted and believed in, and why, she could not help feeling that there were bounds beyond which she did not desire to proceed, and she refrained from going to extremes. She has not followed in all their new departures and extravagances those new-comers, who grope right and left without being able to make up their minds — a common occurence with youthful people of talent who still lack knowledge and balance. Neither sudden, fleeting currents of fashion, nor the influence of public infatuation and thirst for novelty at all costs, nor the fear to stand impeached for conservatism and lack of daring, have had the slightest influence on her. She has proved capable of evincing interest in innovations, but only in those which bore the stamp not merely of novelty, but also of genuine artistic feeling and taste. Without a sense of proportion and fitness, there can be no true art and no enduring creation.

I am firmly convinced that no dancer of the newer school, fully trained to ignore and to shun " the conventionalities of classical dancing ", could dance with so full a comprehension of the new requirements of her art, of the new tendencies of technique and aesthetics, as Pavlova does in Paul Dukas's Ballet *La Péri*. In the wonderfull setting of an enchanted valley, gorgeous with rare, supernatural flowers, radiant in a mystic violet aurora, she appears, aerial in her slim, supple grace, mysterious, entrancing, carrying in her hand the Blossom of Life, which she guards from Iskander, the young conqueror of Iran, whom she meets roving through the valley. The intricate richness of Paul Dukas's rhythms, his bold melodic patterns, the wealth of harmonic and polyphonic under-currents and contrasts, are things which make the music of *La Péri* call for a most carefully thought out and skilfully carried out choregraphic interpretation.

Here Pavlova appears in a most original light. The whole of her technique has been remodelled and enriched to so great an extent, that some people who thought they knew her thoroughly would hardly believe their eyes, could hardly realise that a classical ballerine would find it possible thus to transform her dancing to the very essence. But the gift of reincarnation does not lie in adherence to " old " tenets any more than it does in adherence to " new " :

it lies in the artistic comprehension of the thing to be achieved, and the capacity to achieve it according to its true spirit.

Pavlova has appeared in another non-classical ballet, " The Seven Daughters of the King ", by Fokin, to music by Spendiarof. That work is founded on one of the Tales in the *Arabian Nights;* and Pavlova appears in it as one of the Daughters of the King of the Djinns.

" To guard his daughters against the lures of love, the King keeps them confined within the precincts of a castle built upon the top of an almost inaccessible mountain. And there the seven Princesses lead a dull life, ignorant of all enjoyment.

" In the beautiful gardens provided for them they remain weary, dejected, until the day when Prince Hassan makes his appearance at the gates.

" One of the pretty captives, whose name is " Crystal-Clear-Stream " (Pavlova), proves wisest, and implores her sisters to allow no stranger in. But the others, who yearn for pleasures and excitement, open the gates. Soon the King hears of his daugters misdemeanour, and orders them to perish by fire. Alone Crystal-Clear-Stream is spared : but she cannot endure to be separated from her beloved sisters, and she dies at the dawn of day. "

Pavlova's interpretation of the part is graced with the poetic simplicity of that Eastern legend. Her attitudes, her movements, her restraint and originality make the onlooker wonder that an achievement of that kind should come from her whom the world knows as the classical dancer *par excellence.* The scene of her death by the fountain, in the pale-rose light of dawn, is so brief and simple that it might be described as merely schematic : yet it produces an intense impression, its very simplicity strikes one as the supreme token of genuineness. Pavlova with her great white wings, broken under the weight of her grief, is like a wonderful blossom from afar, crushed by the storm, which we see gently dying by the rippling waters, under the first rays of the kindly sun.

She is a legendary being moving in a subtle and sweet atmosphere of pathos, half human being, half spirit of the air, a creature of wonderful purity whose great white wings will carry her high above the world, when guilty sisters are doomed to remain on earth. And that impression of immaculate chastity, of ethereal grace, is conveyed by Pavlova unspoilt by any colour of impatience or asceticism, beautiful in its gentle resignation and longanimity. Only the greatest artists are capable of such subtlety and fulness in their interpretations.

Photo Hutchinson.

PAVLOVA
IN " THE DUMB MAID OF PORTICI "

Les Trois Pantins de Bois is a mimodram by Pierre Chantel, to music by Michel-Maurice Lévy. Pavlova has no dancing part in it : the three puppets do the dancing, she is a little girl watching them from her death-bed :

... Mais vinrent les nuits de décembre ;
La fillette toussa longtemps ;
Personne n'était dans sa chambre.
Ses membres tremblaient, grelottants.

On n'a pas de feu ni de mère,
Quand on est pauvre, auprès de soi !
Et toujours, comme une prière,
Les Pantins entendaient : « J'ai froid ! ».

Alors, pensant qu'une flambée
Réchaufferait ses petits doigts,
A pieds joints dans la cheminée
Ils se jetèrent tous les trois.

" The part of the little girl " writes M. Louis Laloy " is played by Pavlova, who displays most exquisite feeling and achieves, by dint of a virtuosity which can only be described as prodigious, effects of most touching simplicity. See her, broken by illness, clasp to her heart the three Puppets which the Cruel Man, the heartless creditor, is preparing to take away ! How delicate she is in her weakness when she collapses by the fireless hearth ! And at the end, how incorporeal a joy ravishes and transfigures her when she revives, by virtue of the kindly little puppets' sacrifice, for a few instants, only too short for us, during which we see that Quen or dancing dance at last ! "

ANNA PAVLOVA
dans "la Libellule"

PAVLOVA
IN THE " SYRIAN DANCE "
BY AIMÉ STEVENS

DESIGN FOR THE SETTING OF THE SECOND ACT
OF "THE SLEEPING BEAUTY", BY S. SOUDEIKINE

ANNA PAVLOVA
IN " LES SYLPHIDES "
BY VALENTINE-J. HUGO

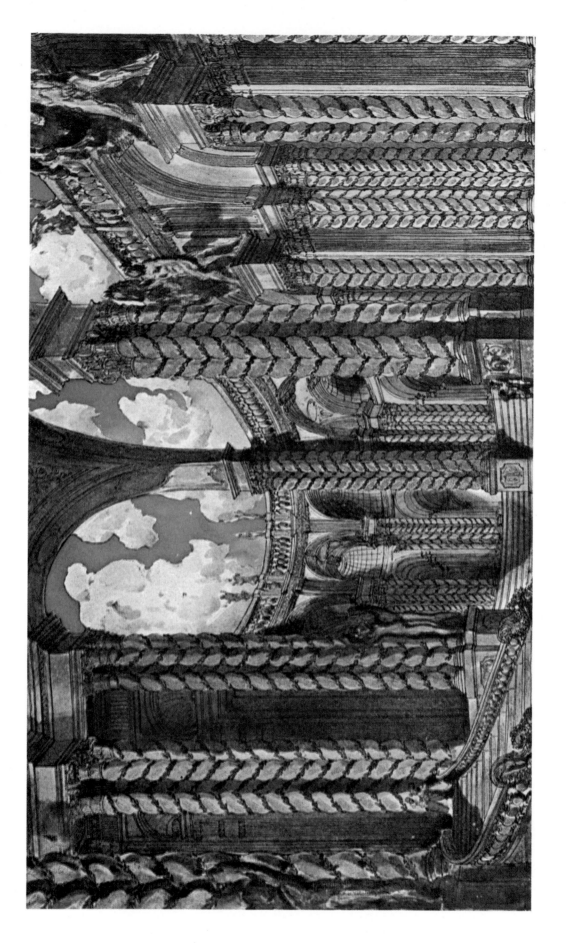

DESIGN FOR THE SETTING OF THE FIFTH ACT
OF "THE SLEEPING BEAUTY BY" LÉON BAKST

DESIGN FOR THE SETTING OF THE "ORIENTAL BALLET"
BY LÉON BAKST

Water-colour drawing of Pavlova's costume
in "The Sleeping Beauty" by Léon Bakst

WATER-COLOUR DRAWING FOR PAVLOVA'S COSTUME
IN "THE KING'S SEVEN DAUGHTERS" BY B. ANISFELD

PAVLOVA
PORTRAIT BY AIMÉ STEVENS

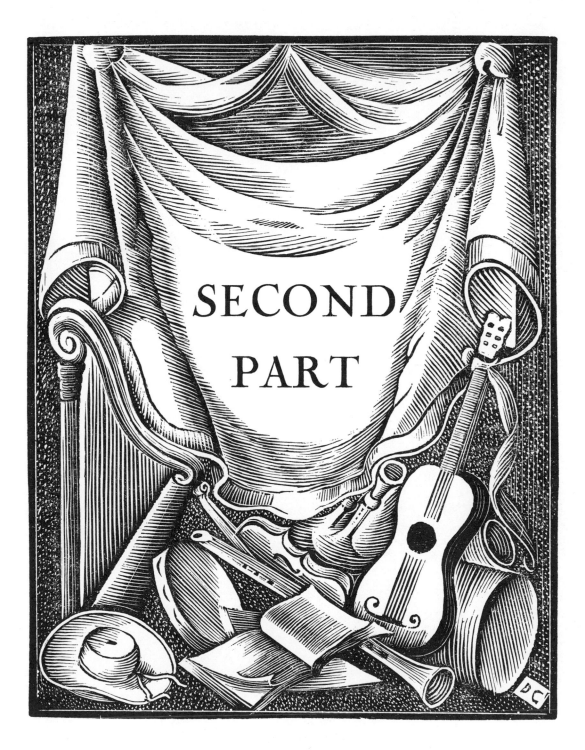

PAGES OF MY LIFE

Translated

by Sébastien Voirol

 IVID are my earliest recollections, which take me back to the time when I was living in a little flat with my mother at Petrograd. I was the only child; and my father having died two years after my birth, we two were alone in the world.

My mother was a most pious woman. She taught me to cross myself and pray in front of the holy *ikôn* in our sitting-room. The Blessed Virgin, whose sweet wistful eyes seemed to look kindly into mine, became a beloved friend. I used to hold conversations with her every morning and every evening, telling her all my infant woes, all my little joys and hopes.

We were poor — very poor indeed; and yet my mother would never fail to provide, on the occasion of feast-days, a surprise for me, in the shape of some treat. For instance, at Easter, I would discover with glee some pretty toys enclosed in a gigantic egg. At Christmas we always had our Christmas-tree, a little fir adorned with golden fruit shimmering with the reflected light of many little candles. And I can still remember my enthusiasm when one day (I was eight years old) I heard that we were to celebrate Christmas by going to see a performance at the Marinsky Theatre.

I had never yet been to the Theatre, and I plied my mother with questions in order to find out what kind of show it was that we were going to see. She replied by telling me the story of the Sleeping Beauty — a favourite of mine among all fairy-tales, and one which she had already told me countless times.

When we started for the Marinsky Theatre, the snow was brightly shining in the reflected light of street-lamps and shop-windows. Our sleigh was noiselessly speeding along the hard surface, and I felt unspeakably happy, seated beside my mother, her arm tenderly enclosing my waist. " You are going to enter fairyland " said she, as we were being whirled across the darkness towards the theatre, that mysterious unknown.

THE FIRST CALL OF THE VOCATION

The music of the " Sleeping Beauty " is by our great Tchaïkovsky. As soon as the orchestra begun to play, I became very grave and attentive, eagerly listening, moved for the first time in my life by the call of Beauty. But when the curtain rose, displaying the golden hall of a wonderful palace, I could not withhold a shout of delight. And I remember hiding my face in my hands when the old hag appeared on the stage in her car driven by rats.

In the second act a swarm of youths and maidens appeared, and danced a most delightful waltz.

— " How would you like to dance thus? " asked my mother with a smile.

— " Oh ", I replied, " I should prefer to dance as the pretty lady does who plays the part of the Princess. One day, I shall be the Princess, and dance upon the stage of this very theatre ".

My mother muttered that I was her silly little dear, and never suspected that I had just discovered the idea that was to guide me throughout my life.

When we left the theatre, I was living in a dream. During the journey home, I kept thinking of the day when I should make my first appearance on the stage, in the part of the Sleeping Beauty.

— " Darling mother, " I said as soon as we had reached home " you will have me taught to dance, won't you? "

— " Yes, certainly, my little Nura (that was her pet name for

ANNA PAVLOVA
Pierrette

PAVLOVA
AT THE AGE OF TWELVE

me), I shall'' she replied, kissing me, and no doubt thinking of the joy she would experience in seeing me waltz at the time when, having reached a marriageable age, I should be taken out into society.

But it was not of society nor of ball-rooms that I was dreaming. All my thoughts were centred on the Ballet. That very night, I dreamt that I was a Ballerina, and spent my whole life dancing, like a butterfly, to the sounds of Tchaïkovsky's lovely music. I love to remember that night, which was to be the prime mover of my career, with all the joys and pains which it was to bring me.

The next morning I could speak of nought but of my great resolve. Then my mother began to understand that her daughter was a most earnest and determined little person.

— '' In order to become a dancer '' she said '' you will have to leave your mother and become a pupil of the Ballet school. My little Nura would not like to forsake her mama, would she? Most certainly not! ''

— '' No, I replied, '' I have no wish to leave you, mama dear.

PAVLOVA
IN THE " MEXICAN DANCE "

But if it is necessary for me to part with you in order to become a Ballerina, I shall have to resign myself to it ". And, kissing her, I begged her to secure my admission to the school.

She refused, and I began to weep. It was only a few days later, wondering at my firmness of purpose, that she complied with my desire, and took me to see the Director of the school.

We were, as I said, extremely poor. And it was perhaps in the hope of providing for me at a time when she would no longer be with we, and when I should have to make my way alone and unassisted, that she decided upon that interview — no doubt a great sacrifice on her part.

— " The regulations de not allow us to admit eight-year-old children " the director said. " Bring her back when she will have completed her tenth year. "

And so I had two years to wait — two years during which I remained sad and dreamy, haunted as I was by the desire to become a Ballerina as soon as possible.

I ENTER THE BALLET SCHOOL

According to the custom of those who live at Petrograd, we used to spend our summers in the country, not far from town. It was always a pleasure for me to see our belongings, chair and tables and beds and crockery and kitchen implements (not forgetting the big samovar) packed in a van and carried to the *dacha*, the wooden cottage no bigger than a doll's house. In Russia, when one is in the country, one is allowed to live according to one's fancy. And we elected to spend practically the whole of our days in our verandah. It is there we took our meals; and there my mother used to make me read Krylof's Fables aloud, or teach me to sew.

Bareheaded, and clad in an old cotton frock, I often would explore the woods close by the cottage. I enjoyed the mysterious aspect of the cloister-like alleys under the fir-trees, all peopled with dancing butterflies. I sought out the most secluded spots, and would sit under a shady tree to build in the air the fragile castles of my dreams.

At times I wove myself a wreath of wild flowers, and imagined myself to be the Beauty asleep in her enchanted castle.

On my tenth birthday, I told my mother that the time had come again to call on the Director of the school. She looked very grave, but did as I had asked her.

FREDMANN-CLUZEL
PAVLOVA'S FOOT

I shall not attempt to describe my rapture when the Director promised to secure my admittance to the school. Nevertheless, I shed tears when the day came upon which I had to take leave of my mother. She too wept. I did not understand the reason of her tears, as I understand it now. I was relinquishing the happy peaceful life of home, under the protection of the silver Virgin, and entering the very trying, intoxicating life of a widely different world, the world of art and of the stage. She realised that there could be henceforth no turning back, and that was why she felt sad : for, although one may fail to find happiness in theatrical life, one never wishes to give it up after having once tasted its fruits.

To enter the school of the Imperial Ballet is to enter a convent whence frivolity is banned, and where merciless discipline reigns.

Every morning at eight, the solemn tolling of a big bell would put an end to our sleep. We dressed under the stern eyes of a governess, whose duty is was to see that all hands were kept perfectly clean, all nails in good trim, and all teeth carefully washed. When we were ready, we went to prayers, which were sung by one of the older pupils in front of an ikôn underneath which a tiny flickering lamp was burning like a little red star. At nine, breakfast — tea, bread and butter — was served, and immediately after the dancing lesson began.

We were all gathered in a big room, very high and well lit. There was no furniture except a few benches, a piano, and enormous mirrors. The walls were decorated with portraits of Russia's sovereigns. After the small novices' lesson, the elder, more advanced pupils had their turn, and the beginners withdrew to another room, where they pursued their work.

At twelve, the bell rang for lunch, after which we were taken out for a walk. Then more exercises until four o'clock, and then dinner. After dinner, we enjoyed a period of leisure. Then came fencing lessons, music lessons, and from time to time rehearsals of dances, which were to be performed on the stage of the Marinsky Theatre. When we children had to appear in a Ballet, we were taken to the theatre in great, well-closed cars. Supper used to be at eight, and an hour later we were sent to bed. On feast-days, we were taken to one of the Imperial Theatres : at times to the Theatre Michel, to see French plays performed by the French artists belonging to the Imperial company.

The most exciting days in our well-ordered life were those when the Emperor paid a visit to the school. In those times the Imperial family used to mark their interest in the school by frequent visits. And then, to please the Empress, the children would perform a Ballet on the school's little stage.

I can remember that one day, when I was a little girl, the Emperor Alexandre and the Empress Maria, with other members of the Imperial family, came to see one of those performances. At the end of the Ballet we were allowed to go into the auditorium. The Tsar took my little comrade, Stanislava Belinskaya, in his arms. He was so kind-hearted and unaffected, in all respects a true Russian! At that very instant, I burst into tears. Naturally I was asked why I wept. And between two sobs I replied, with tears trickling fast down my cheeks :

" I want the Emperor to take me into his arms too! " Grand Duke Vladimir, in order to comfort me, took me upon his knee. But I was not satisfied, and went on weeping and repeating " I want the Emperor to kiss me! " The Grand Duke laughed heartily.

After the performance, the Imperial family would come to the dining-room and have tea with us. We were not in the least embarrassed by their presence. The Emperor and Empress were so kind, so very much like a kind father and mother, that we were quite at ease with them, and altogether content.

Every Sunday my mother came to see me; and I used to spend all my holidays with her. During the summer we always lived in the country. We grew so fond of our little holiday cottage, that even now we have not the heart to give it up in favour of some more comfortable abode. And I am writing these pages upon a table on the verandah, amidst surroundings which I love because every feature reminds me of the days of my childhood.

I BECOME " PREMIÈRE DANSEUSE "

I left the Ballet School at the age of sixteen; and shortly afterwards, I was permitted to style myself " Première Danseuse " — which is an official title, exactly as that of " tchinovnik " in goverment offices. Later I was granted the title of Ballerina, which only four other dancers of the present time have received.

After reading Taglioni's life, I conceived the notion of dancing in foreign countries — for the celebrated Italian used to appear everywhere. She danced at Paris, at London and in Russia, where she is still remembered. A cast of her little foot is preserved at Petrograd.

One of the first exercises which the would-be dancer has to perform is to stand on tip-toe. At first, the child can hardly remain in that position for more than a second : but methodical training gradually strengthens the muscles of her toes, so that after a time she is able to make a few steps — clumsily at first, and very much after the fashion of a tyro skater; then, in proportion as she acquires proficiency, the little dancer learns to walk on tip-toe as easily as a violinist performs a scale on his instrument.

After having mastered that first difficulty, the pupil has to get acquainted with steps of all kinds. The teacher performs a few steps; then half-a-dozen children imitate his movements as best they can, for ten minutes, while the others watch. Then the little performers

Photo Van Riel.

PAVLOVA AND STOWITZ
IN " LA PÉRI "

are allowed to rest, and others take their place.   Apart from numer-
ous, varied and complicated steps which belong to the classical ballet,
one has to learn a quantity of national and historical dances : the
Minuet, the Mazurka, Hungarian, Italian, Spanish dances, and so
forth.

As is the case in all branches of art, success depends in a very
large measure upon individual initiative and exertion, and cannot be
achieved except by dint of hard work.   Even after having reached
perfection, a Ballerina may never indulge in idleness.   If she wishes

Photo Van Riel.

PAVLOVA AND STOWITZ
IN " LA PÉRI "

to preserve what she has acquired, she must practise her exercises every day, exactly as the pianist has to practise his scales. For the dancer must feel so perfectly at ease so far as technique is concerned, that when on the stage she need devote to it not a single thought, and may concentrate upon expression, upon the feelings which must give life to the dances she is performing.

Equal care must be devoted to acquiring the art of dancing with a partner, which is something quite special and apart. The Ballerina must learn how to assume graceful postures in endless variety, to avoid conveying an impression of monotony which would induce

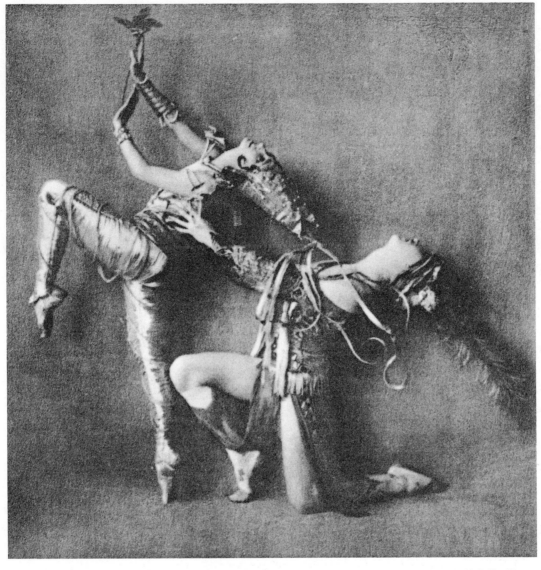

Photo Van Riel.

PAVLOVA AND STOWITZ
IN " LA PÉRI "

weariness : for instance, when after each of her pirouettes her partner catches her in his arms.   All this again calls for constant practice and no small variety of exercises.

At the School of the Imperial Ballet, the history of the art of dancing is now included in the curriculum, and is one of the matters set for the yearly examinations.   The art of making-up is taught with very special care and thoroughness : for a dancer is naturally expected to be capable of appearing at will as a Spanish maiden, or Chinese, or Greek, not to mention dozens of other types.

My first tour began with Riga, in 1907. That town, with its winding streets and its gothic buildings, is German, not Russian. I arrived with a company, and we performed two Ballets at the Opera-House.

The good Germans of Riga welcomed us so warmly, that I felt encouraged to extend the scope of my tour. So from Riga we went to Helsingfors, Stockholm, Copenhagen, Prag and Berlin. Everywhere our dancing was hailed as the revelation of an art so far unknown.

At Stockholm, King Oscar attended our show every evening, which of course gratified me highly. Nevertheless, I was deeply surprised when one day a chamberlain came to inform me that the king wished to see me at the palace. One of the royal carriages was sent for me, and I drove through the streets of the capital as if I was a real princess. The king received me in an immense room which I had already seen when visiting, as all tourists do, the Royal Palace. He made a little speech, very kind and charming, to thank me for the pleasure which my dancing had given him. He also granted me the emblem of the Swedish order " Litteris et Artibus ". He told me that he liked the dances of Southern Europe above all things; and that of all the dances which he had seen me perform, it was a Spanish one which he preferred.

I fully appreciated the Sovereign's most flattering graciousness; but I was even more deeply delighted by the spontaneous tribute of the big crowd that one night assembled, and paid me the compliment of escorting me from the theatre to the hotel.

There are people who refuse to believe that a dancer's life can be otherwise than frivolous. But in fact, the dancer's profession is altogether incompatible with a frivolous mode of living. If a dancer, yielding to temptation, ceases to exercise over herself the strictest control, she will find it impossible to continue dancing. She must sacrifice herself to her art. Her reward will be the power to help those who come to see her to forget a while the sadnesses and monotony of life.

That much I realised, for the first time, at Stockholm.

In the crowd which escorted me when I left the theatre, there were people of all stations: men and women belonging to the middle-class *bourgeoisie*, clerks and workmen, dressmaker's hands, shop assistants. They were all following my car, silently, and then remained standing in front of my hotel until I was told that they wished me to show myself on the balcony. As soon as they saw me, they greeted me with a stormy outburst of cheers which, coming after

ANNA PAVLOVA

Sanguine de Jacovleff

the deep, protracted silence, sounded almost alarming. I bowed my head to them from time to time; and all of a sudden, they started singing national tunes in my honour. I stood vainly seeking for a way of expression my gratefulness to them. Then an idea struck me. I turned into my room, and came back with the wreaths and baskets of flowers which had been handed to me on the stage. But even after I had thrown roses and lilies and violets and lilacs to the crowd, they seemed loth to retire. I was deeply moved and quite embarrassed. I could not help asking my maid : " But what have I done to move them to so great an enthusiasm? "

" Madam, " she replied " you have made them happy by enabling them to forget for an hour the sadnesses of life. "

I never forgot those words. By speaking thus, my maid, a simple Russian peasant girl, gave me a new goal for my art.

MY TOUR THROUGH AMERICA

The following year I went with a Russian company to Leipzig, Prag, and Vienna. We were dancing Tchaïkovsky's beautiful " The Swans' Lake. " Later I joined Mr Diaghilef's company, in order to show Paris the art of the Russian Ballet. Mr Fokin, the ballet-master, succeeded in pleasing the Parisians, who have so refined and so critical an understanding of art. He is a man of genius; and I am delighted that he should have succeeded at Covent-Garden too.

Yet, the beauty of the scenes he combines, the splendours of the setting and costumes, the charm of the music, exercise so captivating and surprising an effect upon the public, that the dancers individuality is lost sight of. Therefore Paris, whilst acquainted with the Russian Ballet in the form given to it abroad by Fokin's genius, does not know me as England and America do.

During the course of that season in Paris, I crossed the channel in order to dance at a reception given by Lady Londersborough in the honour of King Edward and Queen Alexandra. Their Majesties were graciously pleased to express their thanks for the pleasure which they had taken in my dances.

I returned to London in 1910, in order to appear at the Palace Theatre. Several friends had warned me that a first-class dancer belonging to the Imperial Ballet should not appear on the stage of a music-hall. But I knew the London public and the London theatres so well, that not for one instant did I hesitate to sign a contract binding me to appear at the Palace. And I never had cause to regret having signed it.

The British public is most kind and sensitive. It has always been a great joy for me to find that British audiences evince a marked preference for the very dances I like best, and in which I give the utmost and best that is in me. I have the feeling now that perfect understanding exists between the British public and myself.

A tour to America, in the course of which I danced at the Metropolitan Opera, New-York, followed my London season. Naturally, I was delighted with the welcome I found in that country. The newspapers published portraits of me, essays on my art, interviews, and, to tell the whole truth, yarns of all kinds concerning my life, my tastes, my ideas. I have had many a good laugh reading those extraordinarily fanciful articles, and discovering in them that I am the strangest and queerest person on the whole world. The American journalist may indeed be proud of his marvellous imagination.

After New-York, our tour carried us through various States. It was a triumphal march, but an exceedingly fatiguing one. We lived in the special train which was taking us from one place to another across thousands of miles of country. Sometimes we would arrive at a certain spot with just time enough to go from the train to the theatre for the performance. Hardly did the performance end, that we rushed post-haste back to the train, which whirled us away throughout the night (and perhaps the following day as well) towards some other town where a performance was due. It was desired that I should return to America the following year, and I longed to do so : but I lacked the physical energy to repeat so arduous a journey across the New Continent. The ordeal is far too trying to the nerves.

We stayed at little towns in Canada : at Vancouver among other places. An incident which took place there, though trifling, amused me greatly ; it illustrates the delightful courtesy of the Canadians.

After having danced at the theatre, I wished to go and have some supper at a restaurant. I found every table occupied, and not one seat vacant. Several people, having recognised me, offered their seats to me ; and I was feeling so tired that in the end I accepted one. When I had finished my meal, a gentleman who was seated at another table stood up, and in an extemporised speech asked all present to drink my health.

His kind attention pleased me greatly. But I remember that my chief concern was for the old travelling suit which I was wearing — I am not ashamed to acknowledge as much : any woman would have felt the same under similar circumstances. But my old clothes did not stand me in bad stead : all responded to the invitation, and drained their glasses in my honour.

The next day, the incident was described in the newspapers.

A GROUP OF ANNA PAVLOVA'S PUPILS

The Americans, eager not to be outdone in the matter of courtesy, paid me a similar compliment at Portland.

ART THE SOLE MASTER OF MY LIFE

I had spoken so much about myself, that I think I may continue a while, in order to reply to a question which is often made to me. In my opinion a true artist must devote herself wholly to her art. She has no right to lead the life which most women long for.

...The wind rustles through the branches of the fir-trees in the forest opposite my verandah, the forest through which, as a child, I longed to rove. The stars shine in the evening gloom. I have come to the end of these few recollections. While writing them down, I started realising more fully the purpose of my life and its unity. To tend, unfailingly, unflinchingly towards a goal, is the secret of success. But success? what exactly is success? For me it is to be found not in applause, but in the satisfaction of feeling that one is realising one's ideal. When, a small child, I was rambling over there by the fir-trees, I thought that success spelt happiness.

I was wrong. Happiness is like a butterfly which appears and delights us for one brief moment, but soon flits away.

ANNA PAVLOVA.

AT THE PETROGRAD THEATRE MARIE

 ONG after leaving school, Pavlova continued to improve her technique under the guidance of the best teachers. Oblakof, Ivanof, Iohansen, Gherdt, Cecchetti, the Italian Ballerina Signora Baretta and the Russian Ballerine Vasem and Sokolova assisted her during the course of her artistic career.

Whilst assimilating the technique and methods of her masters, Pavlova was very careful not to follow blindly the path of consecrated doctrines, nor the routine of any of the various schools. She paid the greatest attention to the teaching and advice of all, and followed both; but only in order to assimilate their tuition in altogether individual wise, in accordance with the impulses of her own talent.

For natures less gifted and less original, faultlessly to reproduce what the teacher holds out as a model is the ideal. But Pavlova, in her evolution as an artist, proceeded otherwise : when assimilating, she did not imitate; she transformed.

Her great talent enabled her to alter in full independence, and after

PAVLOVA AND FOKIN
IN " HARLEQUINADE "

her own fashion, all the various elements suggested by her masters.

— " No, you haven't got it at all right! " one of her old teachers used to say to her during lesson-time. " And yet, what you are doing is so original, so very much your own, that I should hardly be justified in insisting that you should do it otherwise. "

Despite the all-powerful traditions of the Imperial stage, when

WATER-COLOUR DRAWING FOR PAVLOVA'S COSTUME
IN " THE SWANS' LAKE " BY LÉON BAKST

she left school, she did not find herself relegated, according to custom, to the last ranks of the corps-de-ballet.   Her talents were so obvious, that there could be no question of enforcing the rule which applied to beginners.   Instead, she was entrusted at first with a few small

DIATCHKOFF
WATER-COLOUR DRAWING FOR PAVLOVA'S COSTUME IN THE " SPANISH DANCE "

parts.   Then she was allowed to appear in small one-act Ballets, although such a course of procedure was an infringement of both regulations and tradition.

Here are a few of the minor parts and soli entrusted to Pavlova in the course of her first years of dancing upon the imperial stage : Hulnare in *The Corsair;* Sister Anna in *Blue Beard;* La Fée Candide, la Fée des Canaries, and Princess Florine in *The Sleeping Beauty;* Fleur de Lys's little friend in *Esmeralda;* Juanita in *Don*

Quixote; Henriette in *Raymonda;* Ephemeride in *The Brook;* the Spanish Girl in *La Fée des Poupées.*

After that she appeared in small Ballets. It is in *Flora's awakening* that she made her first debut in an independent part (that of Flora). And possibly it is to the fond recollection of that fact that the maintenance of the aforenamed Ballet in her repertory of to-day is due, as well as that of *The Magic Flute* (in which she first appeared as Lisa).

Giselle was her first big creation on the Imperial stage. To what she did with the title-part, then and after, I have devoted a separate chapter.

This first important attempt had among its other consequences that of winning a place for her in the cast of *La Bayadère*, a big Ballet comprising a wealth of dances and mimic or dramatic scenes.

The critics, as is usual in the case of a newcomer filling a difficult part, observed a cautious reserve; but they did not altogether refrain from showing sympathy and approval. It is especially with the public that Pavlova's success was great.

Hardly had she perfected in all its details the part of the dancing-girl Nicaea, that the part became the most precious gem in the set of all those which she filled at Petrograd.

She had a perfect knowledge of the score, which is, from the point of view of technique, extremely intricate. Every one of her dances, every one of her attitudes, each movement and step of hers proved remarkable for its refinement and beauty, and reminded one of the finest things to be seen in statuary. In the dramatic passages, she was the very soul of eloquence, and her miming was instinct with tragic impressiveness.

The critics acknowledged at last that Pavlova's performance in *La Bayadère* was a display of that live flame which characterises all the doings of a true artist. It was realised that she was introducing in her art something specifically her own, something altogether different from what had been seen before.

In "the Kingdom of the Shadows" (the fourth scene in *La Bayadère*) her appearance constitues the most impressive of visions. After Nicaea's death, occasionned by the sting of a snake which a rival has hidden in a basket of flowers, her soul is carried to the Valley of the Dead. It is in that mysterious world, the realm of eternal moon-light, that her pellucid wraith is seen by us.

That act is a wonder. Mystical poetry and lyrical charm, combined with perfect choregraphy, produce a peerless impression of

PAVLOVA AND HER PEKINESE

perfect harmony and style.   Pavlova's technique is as remarkable for its distinction as for its brilliancy, and her creation of that part is no lesser thing than her *Giselle*.

There is a degree of analogy between the Willis in *Giselle* and the shadows in *La Bayadère*.   Both Ballets are founded on the romance of a young maiden, deceived in her love, who falls a victim to her very purest feelings.   Both show the maiden resurrected in the mysterious world of dreams and fancies.

But between the two there are a number of dissimilar features subtle enough to remain unnoticed by many dancers.   With surpassing perceptiveness, Pavlova takes into account every one of those elusive shades which differentiate the romanticism of the 'forties from the exotic colour of *La Bayadère*.

After *La Bayadère* came a third great part for Pavlova : in the Ballet *Paquita*.

That Ballet represents Spain in a romantic aspect; but its romanticism is spurious, theatrical, altogether conventional, and has nothing to do with true Spain. It is only in recent times that Spanish dances have been performed on the stage in accordance with that country's genuine tradition. Up till now, the custom was to arrange them and colour them with special characteristics, giving them the appearance of so many conventional " stage-turns ", partly choregraphic, partly of the kind customary on the music-hall stage.

It is hardly to be wondered that Pavlova should have found it difficult to contend with that routine, which tradition had strongly established. Yet, so far as was possible, she succeeded in giving new life and new beauty to her dances in that part.

Her variations in the *Boléro* style impressed the public deeply, for in them she displayed wonderful grace and suppleness. Then came a " Spanish Step " to show how fully she had mastered the spirit and methods of folk-dancing. But it was especially in the " Grand Pas " — that masterpiece among Petipa's inventions — that she proved matchless. No other dancer before her, and none after her, has proved able to perform classical Spanish dances with equal elegance, suppleness, nimbleness and brilliancy.

M. Andreevsky, the Russian poet, has said of her : " Her dancing resembles the vibrating flight of a tone from the string of a harp ".

Pavlova seems to have been born for Spanish dances, and endowed with the very gift of rendering their style, their poses so full of haughty pride and gracefully curved lines. Her elegant suppleness provides an inexhaustible variety of beautiful attitudes, tense or relaxed. Her " entrechats ", her " développés " are supremely fine; her " envolés " and " cabrioles " full of spirit and ease. She never lets one single movement impair the harmony between her torso and her arms. Her dances are a fautless oblation to the cult of beautiful lines and sculptural attitudes.

From the dramatic point of view, her rendering of the part of Paquita calls for no lesser praise.

In it she introduces, so far as classical art permits, an element of realism : and as she conceives it, so she performs it, with that perfect understanding of the principles of beauty which knows where the line should be drawn. And she experiences no difficulty in so doing. In the scene in the tavern, the mimic action is wonderfully interwoven in the very texture of the dancing, and the two elements together appear in a unique combination. The impression which that

KOROVIN
WATER-COLOUR DRAWING FOR PAVLOVA'S COSTUME IN THE "RUSSIAN DANCE"

scene produces is something which those who have seen it will never forget, so glowingly does Pavlova assert her temperament in it, so full of life are her beautiful attitudes, gestures, and dances.

Imitating nobody, affected by no influence, Pavlova followed her

ANNA PAVLOVA
Statuette by de Boulongne

way, led and moved by a talent which was clearly progressing towards fuller development. Every part which she created bore the stamp of her original and powerful individuality. And within an incredibly short space of time, she scored a triad of triumphant successes, leaving forever her mark upon the three creations of *Giselle*, *La Bayadère* and *Paquita*.

In Medora *(The Corsair)* a Ballet derived from Byron's poem, Pavlova has provided a romantic silhouette of a sort which is delightful as much by virtue of its general character as through the minute skill and refinement shown in the carrying out of every detail.

She is, unquestionably, the best exponent of that part, consisting entirely of colour and miming in the settings of a Ballet filled to repletion with romantic adventures, and the best possible. Far from underlining the somewhat crude elements supplied by the libretto, she contrives artistically to relegate them to the background. Thus, in the rather risky scene in the cavern, she adapts certain details so as to render the scene more subtle and neater than it was in the realistic interpretation previously adopted. She gives us a touching picture of Medora, a picture instinct with poetic charm.

The very style of the dances in *The Corsair* is in perfect agreement with Pavlova's choreographic manner. They are graceful, aerial, conceived in a spirit of virtuosity, and their complexity affords a great scope for technical proficiency.

Confident in her powers, Pavlova performs them gracefully and with perfect ease. All the requisite qualities are displayed by her from the outset to the finish, from the flying leaps when she enters to the various passages in the *Finesse d'amour* (Pas d'Action), in which she asserts coquettish grace in countless delightful ways. In the " Pas de Deux " her " renversés ", at the end of which she gracefully falls upon her knees, are pure marvels. The same may be said of that variation of hers founded upon the " fouettés en diagonale " a step technically most difficult, but far more beautiful than the ordinary " fouetté ". And there is in *The Corsair* another passage worthy of notice, one which constitutes a charming tableau de genre, with Pavlova in male attire : *The little Corsair*, a dance devoid of complications, but which calls for discriminating and refined taste.

In " The Live Garden ", a scene to music by Delibes introduced in *The Corsair*, the public is enabled to admire Pavlova's " cabrioles ", ample, easy and beautifully outlined.

We have described, so far as was possible, the subject of the romantic Ballet *Paquita* interpreted by Pavlova. Remains to say a few words about *Don Quixote*, which is a kind of pantomime in up-to date style belonging to the repertory of the Theatre Marie.

Pavlova appeared in it in the part of Kitry. As that part comprises no miming, she is at liberty to concentrate upon dancing proper. And it is wonderful to see her yielding, unreservedly and unhampered, to the spirit of pure dancing. She reveals to the fullest extent the charm and grace of her art, expressed in what can best be described as a dream of harmony and beauty.

Her achievement is all the more remarkable when it is realised how great the technical difficulties are which she has to overcome in the "notes piquées" of Kitry's Dance, in its "envolés" and "développés". But that technical aspect of her performance remains unnoticed, for she veils it in yon sublime beauty which is, in Schiller's words, "the harmony of dream".

Before appearing in the big part of Kitry, she had been allotted that of Juanita, the seller of fans. Although it was but a little part, she was able to assert the greatness of her talent in it. But nobody thought that soon after, she was to be entrusted with the principal part in the same ballet. Yet a few critics had foretold it.

Kitry's dances delighted the very fastidious Petrograd public. The critics were no less pleased. They were surprised with Pavlova's progress in classical technique, they praised the excellence of her capers in the Dancing Scene, the brightness of her "jetés" and variations, the improvement in her "ballon". Every day brought additional grace and finish to her attitudes and movements.

Among the Ballets of the old repertory which the Ballet-Master Gorsky revived at Moscow, a special mention should go to *Pharao's Daughter*.

It is at the Moscow Imperial Theatre that Pavlova had been engaged for a series of special performances. The public of that theatre have their own taste, and are very hard to please : yet they approved of Pavlova from the very outset. This in itself constituted for her a not inconsiderable success : for the conservative spirit of Moscow was not inclined to favour what came from elsewhere — and especially from Petrograd.

But very characteristic was the way in which the Moscovites acknowledged Pavlova's talent. They praised her plastical gifts, her comprehension of the art of dancing, her interpretation of the *Oriental Variations*. In the first part of those *Variations,* they were alive to the charm of her languid attitudes, and in the second to the vigour

PAVLOVA
AFTER A TRIUMPH

of her artistic temperament. The waltz and variations in quick tempo, executed on tip-toe, the *Dance of the Crotals* with its ample leaps and formidable " ballon ", and the brilliancy which she displayed at the head of all the other dancers, won golden opinions from the whole of Moscow. The scene in the Fisherman's hut provided an opportunity to judge of the artist's capacity for dramatic expression : for there Pavlova has to give an account of her adventures — which she does with exquisite spirit and zest, until the moment when the appearance of the King of Nubia pursuing his escaped bride interrupts the delightful scene, and tragedy begins. It is then that Pavlova becomes truly sublime, reaching the utmost depths of pathos, the depths where Beauty becomes almost awesome.

At Petrograd, she danced with no lesser success the same Ballet, staged in somewhat different wise.

But although it has remained included until quite lately in the curent repertory, the Ballet *Pharaos's Daughter* is one of the most archaic of all those which Petipa has produced.

There are other things created by Pavlova on the stage of the Theatre Marie which did not belong to the usual repertory of that stage : things which date from the time when Fokin's innovations were on the point of doing away for good and all with the inveterate conventions of a threadbare routine.

For that great reformer of the Russian Ballet, whose interest centred chiefly in the pantomimic drama, whichever the style and period might be, Pavlova was naturally the ideal interpreter.

Eunice, a dramatic episode founded on Sienkiewicz's novel *Quo Vadis*, was the first Ballet in ancien style produced by Fokin. It was a great success. In the scenes with Petronius and Actaea, Pavlova displayed an impressive dramatic power. Her sense of Greek plastical style, her perfect comprehension and capacity for interpretation, enabled her to achieve a masterpiece with the Dance of the Sevens Veils.

In *Le Pavillon d'Armide*, a ballet in the style of Louis XIV, she appeared as the enigmatic Armide. That part afforded her the opportunity to display all her refined sense of proportion and character is an altogether new light. And nothing could have shown her versatility better than the constrast between Armide and Eunice : after the elegiac figure of the Greek slave, poetically inspired by love, the perfidious, mysterious woman who revels in her magic power and trifles with a young courtier's passion.

I have as yet mentioned only the principal parts in which Pavlova has appeared on the Imperial stage. To the list must be added : Princess Aurora, in *The Sleeping Beauty*, the Mermaid in *The Mermaid and the Fisherman;* the Spanish Girl in *La Fée des Poupées,*

WATER-COLOUR DRAWING FOR PAVLOVA'S COSTUME
IN THE " RUSSIAN DANCE " BY S. SOLOMKO

and mention should be made of her dances *Panaderos* in *Raymonda*, and of her Pas-de-Deux in *Graziella*.

But we need not dwell any longer upon the pleasant task of describing and analysing her creations. We have said enough. We have become acquainted with the chief gems of her artistic diadem. Of those gems some are altogether peerless, others are lesser in size and richness : but all are wonderfully exquisite, and in brilliancy unsurpassed. The reputation which she acquired she built for her-

PAVLOVA AND NIJINSKY
IN " LE PAVILLON D'ARMIDE "

self, unaided, without ever resorting to advertisement or benefiting by favouritism. It is in her own genius that she found the wealth which by dint of labour became a treasure untold.

First the Imperial School, then the Imperial stage fostered her art, which she extended and perfected, watched by an eager public, encouraged by the sympathy with which the critics welcomed her progress. Later, when her talent had reached its climax and she was in full possession of all her resources, she decided to travel through Europe and to America. The old world and the new were unanimous in applauding her talent.

PAVLOVA AND NIJINSKY
IN " LE PAVILLON D'ARMIDE "

Mr. Zigfrid, a Russian art critic, has written a tale entitled " The Queen of Dancing " which he inscribed to Pavlova. From that tale I shall quote the following excerpt :

" One day, a humble family was celebrating the baptism of a baby girl. From another world fairies came to her cradle, bringing the wonderful gifts which they had prepared for her. The first gave her beauty; the second, intelligence; the third, the qualities that uplift the soul; the fourth, will-power. And the fifth, in whose pale winsome face shone large dark eyes, stooped over the cradle and said : " I bring thee the finest gift that can be granted to a mortal being :

the gift to realise the harmony of the world, the harmony which is everywhere to be found. Thou shalt hear it in the ripple of the brook, in the song of the bird, in the barely perceptible rustle of the grass, in the howl of storm and wind. Thou shalt discover it in the sweetness of moonlight, in the shadow of the mountains, in the uproar of the cities of men... It is the sweetest and the loftiest music : thou shalt learn to understand it, and thus become a poet. Indeed, I bring the power to understand the harmony of the universe. This harmony thou wilt embody in the poetry of thy limbs, in the rhythm of thy motions. Upon inaccessible peaks, aglow with golden light, thou shalt build the mystery of thy palace; and all peoples shall bow to thee in ecstasy ".

" Having spoken those words, the fairy slowly moved her wand thrice around the cradle. Then they all vanished.

" Years elapsed, the child grew, and what the fairies had foretold happened. For she became the queen and poet of dancing; and the whole world, enraptured, acknowledged the Beauty which she came to reveal ".

I have already stated that any attempt to explain talent in terms of science is doomed to failure. The only language in which that can be attempted is that of the fairy-tales, as Mr. Zigfrid has done, describing this language as the most precious gift from the Gods.

But if the art of penetrating the harmony of the universe does not depend upon human will, yet it is true that the capacity to embody that harmony in plastic rhythms remains entirely dependent upon the endowments and exertions, physical and intellectual, of the artist who succeeds in so doing.

And it is in that respect that it may be said of Pavlova : she herself has created her crown of glory and placed it upon her brows.

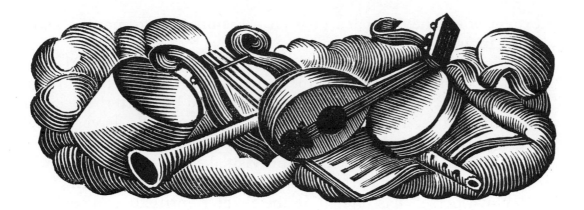

HER TRAVELS

LEARLY, the full chronicle of Pavlova's travels would be too long to include in this volume: for, with her company, she has made the round of all principal centres in the old world and the new.

It is some twelve years ago that Pavlova became known abroad for the first time. Any artist might well envy the reputation which she has acquired since that time. Europe and America have acknowledged her as the greatest and most perfect dancer of our times. Whole continents have hailed her with titles such as *Queen of Dancing* and *Pavlova the Peerless*.

Those travels have had another important result besides revealing her talent to the European and American public: they have helped to acquaint both those continents with Russia's art.

From that point of view, Pavlova's achievements, conducted with untiring energy and spirit, are even more than a mere artistic undertaking, however grand in itself: they constitute a work of propaganda which has attracted towards Russian art special attention and impassioned interest on the part of the public and art-centres of two whole continents. All those people, previously, knew nothing of Russian art except what they had learnt from occasional performances given by Russian artists on tour.

Having studied the Ballets of Paris, Vienna, Berlin and Milano, Pavlova was convinced of the superiority, in more respects than one, of the Russian Ballet. That conviction inspired her with the decision to show that Ballet abroad. She was granted a month's leave, formed a company, and started on her first expedition.

Stockholm was the first city she visited; and the Swedes, who are not easily moved to enthusiasm, were conquered forthwith.

Pavlova herself has related, in the chapter entitled " Pages of my life ", the flattering welcome and the high distinction given her by the King of Sweden.

Thence she went to Copenhagen, where she was equally admired by the Danish court and the whole public.

The third capital to receive her visit was Berlin, where her debut was hailed as a great artistic event. It assumed the character of a genuine revelation, recognised by endless applause and cheers. Painters and sculptors, artists and authors, struggled for the privilege of witnessing her rehearsals, in order to study at leisure her attitudes and movements. On the occasion of her last appearance, the Kroll-Theater became the scene of wild outburst of enthusiasm. Soon afterwards she was offered an engagement at the New York Metropolitan Opera House for the following season.

Her first campaign had ended in complete victory. She returned to Russia, and the following year undertook another tour, beginning with Berlin, Dresden, Prag and Vienna.

At Paris, she made her first appearance at the Théâtre du Châtelet, in Diaghilef's Russian Ballets. The " City of Light " (La Ville-Lumière) ungrudgingly granted its precious endorsement to the praises which had hitherto marked Pavlova's progress, and acknowledged her as a great tragic actress and the first dancer of the times.

Her début in London, at a reception given in honour of King Edward VII, was described in a previous chapter. The British Sovereign was highly pleased. Shortly afterwards, important contracts were offered to Pavlova by the manager of several London theatres. When she returned to Russia, Pavlova was favoured by special attention on the part of her own sovereign. During the course of a performance, the Tsar commanded her to come to his box, and congratulated her for her propaganda in favour of Russian art abroad. " I have but one fear " he said " and that is, that other countries may some day take you away from Russia for good and all. "

PAVLOVA ON A JOURNEY

The following season, she signed a contract with the New-York Metropolitan Opera House. Her success in America was as great as ever; and all the critics of New-York and Boston spoke of her talent in terms of high praise.

The same thing occured again in London, where she returned, after leaving America, for a four months season at the Palace Theatre. And there she came four years in succession, always welcomed and praised, a favourite of the London public.

During the course of one of her performances, she was received by the Spanish sovereigns, on a visit in London. King Alfonso congratulated her upon her successes. " Above all things ", he said " do

THE ADDRESS FROM THE SPANISH COLONY AT MEXICO

not fail to come to Spain : for no country is fonder of dancing than mine. Believe me, your art will be genuinely appreciated there. ''

At the time when war was declared, Pavlova was in America. In October 1914, she began an extensive tour through the Northern part of the continent, from Canada to Florida and from the Atlantic Ocean to the Pacific.

Hardly was that tour, which covered two seasons, finished, she was engaged at New-York for a period of six months, appearing upon the biggest stage in the world : that of the Hippodrome. Among the plays which she gave there, special mention shoul be made of Tchaïkovsky's " Sleeping Beauty '', which the management produced with surpassing splendour. The decorations and costumes were by Léon Bakst, and over 500 persons appeared on the stage.

When the New-York season had ended, Pavlova undertook her first tour through Central and Southern America. She went to Havana, to Costa-Rica, to Panama, followed the coast of Ecuador, and journeyed through Peru, Chili, Argentina and Brazil.

The welcome extended to her by the Peruvians was particulary warm : the municipal authorities at Lima presented her with a gold plate upon which an address was engraved.   At Valparaiso, Santiago

Photo Ira Hill.

PAVLOVA
IN " THE DRAGON-FLY "

de Chili, Montevideo and Buenos-Ayres, she was hailed with no less enthusiastic favour.

Thence she went to give a number of performances in Venezuela and Puerto-Rico, where she rested a while before starting for a new tour, which began at Para in Brazil.

The Brazilians' admiration and delight proved inexhaustible.   A grand reception in Pavlova's honour was organised by the Scientific Societies; the municipal authorities decreed that a commemorative tablet should be placed on a wall of the Municipal Theatre.

From Para, the company went to Pernambuco, Bahia, Rio-de-

Janeiro and Sao Paulo, returning to Buenos-Ayres to retrace its route step by step northwards, following the itinerary of the first tour reversed. At Panama, Pavlova was compelled to remain three weeks by the lack of means of conveyance. She availed herself of that time to give great performances for the benefit of the American naval forces stationed in the Canal zone.

But as no other chance to leave the spot seemed to be forthcoming, Pavlova decided to continue her journey on board a French steamship carrying a cargo of saltpeter to Santiago-de-Cuba, whose skipper had kindly offered accommodation on deck, no other being available. Pavlova and her company of 65 persons camped on deck, sleeping in the open, at the mercy of rain and wind.

Then came invitations to visit Havana and Mexico. In order to exclude the possibility of unpleasant contingencies in a country then swept by the winds of revolution, President Carranza ordered that the train carrying Pavlova and her company should be guarded by 200 soldiers encamped on the roof of the wagons.

It is in the Mexican capital that Pavlova and the artists in her company had for the first time to dance under unfamiliar conditions, at the altitude of 8000 feet. This inconvenienced them a little during the first few days.

The Mexicans, who deservedly enjoy the reputation of being endowed with a refined taste, gave Pavlova an enthusiastic reception. Her visit to Mexico was marked by a whole series of triumphs. Apart from her performances at the Theatre, she organised, on Sundays, matinée performances at the Plaza de Toros, whose auditorium could accomodate no less than 30000 persons. It is there that she danced for the first time, to the acclamations of a delighted crowd, her famous " Mexican Dances ", whose elements she had found in the traditional dances of the country. Thence Pavlova returned to Benuos-Ayres and Rio-de-Janeiro, to return to Europe in October 1919. On her way back she visited Lisbon, Madrid and Paris.

As we have seen, she took her own company with her on all her tours, a company formed, instructed and managed by herself, which constitutes a matchless ensemble, trained in accordance with the best principles.

*   *
*   *

Wherever she appeared, Pavlova was hailed with enthusiasm. A quantity of journalists used to ply her with questions, in the hope

PAVLOVA
IN THE " SYRIAN DANCE "
BY AIMÉ STEVENS

of finding in her replies an explanation of her talent from the point of view of psychology.

With the modesty and simplicity which are so characteristic of her, she was always ready to supply information and to talk of her art.

Here are her own words :

" Every time I am about to appear on the stage, I experience that particular kind of emotion with which novices and artists appearing for the first time are so well acquainted. In my case, this emotion, instead of decreasing with time, becomes stronger and stronger. For I am increasingly conscious of the fact that my responsibilities grow heavier in proportion as my reputation increases. That feeling of uneasiness, that anxiety and suspense are familiar to me : I always experience them, in Petrograd or abroad.

" I have studied a great deal. I have always devoted care to the improvement of my dancing. And I can quite truthfully say that my successes are due firstly to my ceaseless labour and to the merits of my teachers. Marius Petipa was the first to guide my steps. In that respect, I must say that I have been particularly fortunate.

" As regards new tendencies and developments in the Ballet, my views are perfectly simple : I have the greatest appreciation for Fokin, and believe that of all the reformers of dancing he is the most gifted. He and I followed the same path during the whole of my career in Russia. We made our debut together in Drigo's *Harlequinade*. He used me as " material " for his creations. We were uniformly in agreement, and in quest of new revelations in an art of which we had the same conception.

" In my opinion, it is our duty to accept all that is beautiful in new artistic departures. But at the same time, whe should never lack the courage to stick to all that is excellent in the older forms of art. From that point of view, what Marius Petipa has done is in many respects marvellous. The only misfortune is, that in his days the Ballet was considered, so to speak, as a second-rate art. So far as its music was concerned, for instance, it used to be the field of non-entities. It is only at a later time that great composers, such as Tchaïkovsky and Glazunof, began to take an interest in Ballet-music. And is not music the very soul of the Ballet? Art should not, and cannot remain immovable. Progressive evolution is its law. We owe an immense debt of gratitude to Fokin, who succeeded in introducing innovations in the becalmed regime of our choregraphy. But Fokin's advent was heralded and made possible by Petipa, who was the first to create our school of classical dancing. In order to do well

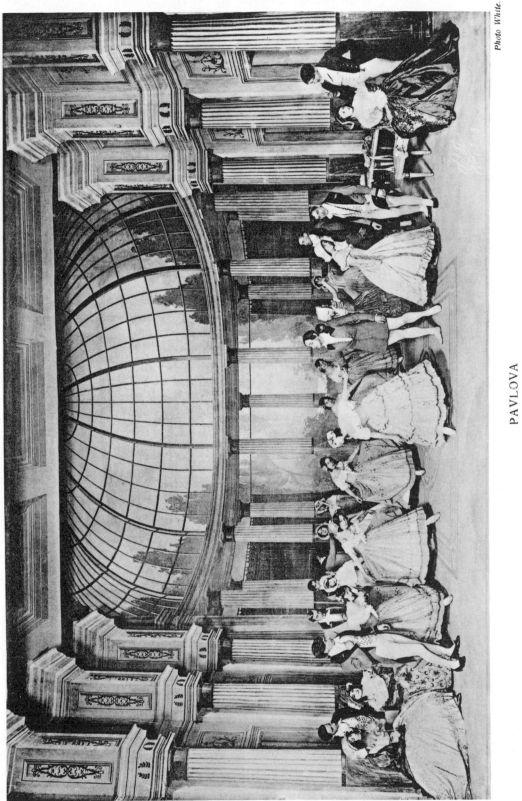

PAVLOVA

IN A SCENE OF " L'INVITATION A LA VALSE "

in the new Ballets, it is necessary to have been fully trained according to the principles of that school.

" Praise has often been bestowed upon my talent. There is no
mystery of any kind in its evolution, since that evolution was accomplished under the eyes of everybody. From a shy, sedulous
pupil, I developed into a dancer at last. But I kept feeling that there
was something imperfect in my art : and what I have been doing since
was to try to remedy it by sedulously developing my capacities.

" But when I felt strong enough, I yielded unreservedly to the
creative impulse which prompted me. Without good, sound tuition
and practice, this would have been impossible. In countries abroad,
it was said that there was " something novel " in my dancing. Yet
what I had done was merely to subordinate its physical elements to a
psychological conception : over the matter-of-fact aspects of dancing
— that is, dancing *per se* — I have attempted to throw a spiritual veil
of poetry, whose charm might screen the mechanical element. When
dancing, it often occurs that I extemporise, especially when my part
fascinates and inspires me. I borrow from the palette of choregraphy
any colour which happens to suit my fancy, and turn the slightest
thing to the best possible account. That is how I may be able to
suggest impressions which are considered as fresh. So far as I know,
therein lies the only secret of my art.

" The British public, which at first had proved somewhat reserved
and almost cold, soon began to reconsider its attitude ; and the
" Palace " became the ground on which Russian artists scored their
most triumphal successes.

" The Londoners, of whom I shall always carry a grateful recollection, welcomed us most cordially, and evinced a keen interest for
our various spectacles. The demand for seats greatly exceeded the
capacity of that fine, but comparatively small theatre. It seems to
me that the British Public has fully realised the poetic merits of
Russian dancing, and knows how to discriminate between it and the
mere mechanical virtuosity which is so often applauded. Generally
speaking, that public's sense for the beautiful is highly developed :
they never commit the mistake of confusing art with mere *métier*.

" Being essentially a lyrical dancer, I was most glad to see that
London preferred that style of dancing to the purely technical.

" Every year, London's interest in the Ballet grows keener, and
the public's sense of art progresses. I know admirers of my Ballets
who came to see them over sixty times.

" There has been a period when no less than four theatres in

PAVLOVA AND VOLININ
IN THE " GAVOTTE "

London were showing artists of the Russian Ballet on their stages : and all four theatres were always full. During one of my London seasons, I conceived the idea to introduce into my repertory an excerpt from the Ballet *Casse-Noisette* in which thirty children appeared on the stage. Those children had been recruited by me from various schools, and received their choregraphic training in six weeks.

" I had the delight of feeling that the audience was highly pleased with the spectacle of all those English children dancing side by side with me.

" The American's nature is more demonstrative : but they too are discriminating, and capable of keeping their appreciation for things which really deserve it. Both the British and Americans arrive at their judgments in full independence — a fact which I greatly appreciate. They never start with preconceived notions. Suggestions made by the Press, and judgments emanating from small groups of artists, do not seem to carry with them the importance which, as I seemed to guess, they carry at times in France. For over there, every one is guided by his or her individual feeling.

" I have sometimes heard people say, that England and America had inadequate notions as regards the art of choregraphy. That is entirely untrue. They are highly cultured people, whose native art stands on a very high level; and accordingly, they have a keen eye for the beautiful; and I should even incline to say that they sometimes display more expert knowledge than others. In the course of my performances, I have had many an opportunity to realise the fact. For instance, I would fear that some detail of my dancing might remain unnoticed by a public which knew little of the special technical points involved : and a moment later, a storm of applause would come to show me that my fears had been altogether unfounded.

" As I have said, the interest evinced by the Americans for Russian art was so genuine and so great, that the railway companies went to the extent of posting special time-tables which showed the inhabitants of the regions around the towns where we were dancing how they could travel to those towns and back. I was greatly moved by attentions of that kind.

" I have danced in the greatest theatres of the United States, beginning with Boston. I have never seen a bigger one; nor have I encountered in the United States a finer and more cultured audience,

" But the taste of the Americans differs to a degree from that of their British cousins. In the United States, the most successful Ballet was *Giselle*.

Design for the setting of "Les Préludes"
by B. Anisfeld

" I was profoundly impressed by California, with its beautiful palm trees and the wild, original character of its scenery.

" It is remarkable that in countries where the heat and sunshine

DESIGN FOR THE SETTING OF " AMARYLLIS "
BY GEORGES BARBIER

are so merciless, the lyrical style should be preferred; whereas in cold climates, it is generally the technical style that enjoys the greater popularity ".

*
* *

Pavlova's successes in all the great cities of the old world and the new, the ovations and praise lavished upon her by critics and poets, have not in the least affected her unassuming simplicity.

We have quoted some of her remarks to pressmen, and the reader will have noticed that she never evinces the slightest tendency to refer to merits of her own. To hear Pavlova speak, one might think her successes entirely due to Russian art and to the contributions of all those who appear as representatives of that art.

Like all true artists, she talks little. She is never eager to supply a purely theoretical explanation of her art. Those who indulge in ceaseless talk about their art are inspired by the conciousness that it is necessary to justify that art in the eyes of the public and critics by some kind of long drawn and far-fetched theory. And in most cases, explanations of that kind leave the public unimpressed, the critics unconvinced, and fail to serve the purpose of those who indulge in them.

As for Pavlova, she creates because it is her vocation to create.

The sedulous care which she devotes to the study of nature has been mentioned above. One of its results is the accurate and perspicuous character of her theoretical conception of her art.

She takes beauty where she finds it. When attempting to find her way into the domain of innovation, she is careful not to display the morbid, unwholesome hurry which is so marked a feature of

PAVLOVA
IN A SCENE OF THE " SYRIAN DANCE "

DESIGN FOR THE SETTING OF " THE KING'S SEVEN DAUGHTERS "
BY BORIS ANISFELD

many so-called innovators in matters of art. She proceeds intel-
ligently, calmly, prudently. She believes that all artistic activities
must proceed from, and rest upon, tradition. An admirer of Michael
Fokin, she is nevertheless aware of all the merits of Petipa, who
founded the old Ballet. She appreciates Isadora Duncan, but is
capable of seeing that the American dancer's art tends to destroy
all that is beautiful in the traditional style of choregraphy.

Such are, in their main lines, Pavlova's theoretical views upon
her art. They are brief and simple indeed, but instinct throughout
with the sense of balance and directness which is one of the chief
elements of the genuine creative spirit.

It is natural enough that her wonderful doings should stimulate
the critics' interest, and stimulate them in their quest for a theory
with which to connect them. But how could a true artist such as
she conduct her creative work in accordance with the tenets of any
preconceived theory? It should not be forgotten that many of the

elements of creation belong to the domain of the unconscious. They are what is generally called the divine afflatus. From the point of view of logic, it is not possible to define nor to explain the impulses to which works of art owe their birth. Indeed, can one perceive and determine the interval between the moment when an image is born within the soul of an artist, and the moment when that image crystallises and expresses itself in tangible form?

The object of talent is to create. That of theory is to study the things created, and to provide elements for their appreciation. Consequently, theory can refer only to things already created.

Her travels have yielded Pavlova a wealth of resources for her imagination to work upon. Those resources she could not have found at home, where the official repertory and time-honoured tradition would have imposed limits upon her eager activity. Russia was for her a preliminary stage. Like a chrysalis, she gradually assumed shape, and stored the power to break from her bonds : and when the time had come, she soared freely in the light of day, a lovely, resplendent butterfly.

THIRD

PART

THE
CRITICS AND PAVLOVA

OUBTLESS it would be a hopeless task to analyse in full all that has been written upon Pavlova and her art. It is actually impossible to enumerate the articles, essays, notices and relations of all sorts, to say nothing of whole volumes in various languages which have been devoted to her throughout the civilised world. Even to give a synthetic conspectus of them, or to summarise their contents in a digest, is not to be attempted.

Yet in a monograph like the present, it is impossible to overlook the rich harvest afforded by that literature of our subject. We shall have to decide upon some kind of limit, so as to render our task feasible. We shall therefore content ourselves with quoting only such opinions expressed by journalists and other writers as refer to the general characteristics of Pavlova's art.

The reader who should like to ascertain what the critics may have had to say with regard to this or that special creation of hers will find the opinions of those critics quoted in the chapters referring to those creations.

The Russian critic M. O. R. writes :

" Pavlova made her appearance in the world of the theatre at a time when everybody had forgotten the very things which for her were the very fundaments and object of art, the things of which she had dreamt since the moment when she entered the artistic career.

" She was convinced that the movements of dancing would some day constitute an incarnation of the pictures she was dreaming of; she held that art would live only when directed by a general conception : her ideal was the choregraphic drama.

" And what did she find instead of that ideal? So called " dramatic " ballets, where crude, incoherent, conventional " acting " took the place of poetic interpretation. All the work done in choregraphy during the second half of the past century suffered from a common defect : it overlooked the very essence of the art. By dint of seeking sensational kaleidoscopic effects, the Ballet-mongers had achieved a medley of incongruous things, of scenes, episodes, and dances, strung together in haphazard wise, according to crude notions of picturesque and exoticism.

" There was no longer a sense of proportion and style, the spirit which gave life to the older Ballets had vanished; and the Ballet itself, as an artistic structure, had ceased to exist after the middle of the nineteenth century. The Ballets themselves vanished; only the talent of the performers remained. No more Ballets : only Ballerine. Smothered under the disproportionate efforts devoted to producing endless, meaningless " turns ", the capacity to create disappeared gradually. The decadence asserted itself, and reached its worst stage during the seventies and eighties.

" Pending the moment when the Ballet was to assert itself in renovated form, Pavlova had to be satisfied with the faint echo of her dreams which a distant past provided. *Giselle,* that time-honoured Ballet of the 'forties, was the only one in which she could discover the elements of a genuine choregraphic drama. By selecting it, she showed the acumen of her instinct as an artist. And thus she revealed the very soul of her art.

" No wonder that she should have been selected to interpret Fokin's conceptions. No wonder that she should have helped him so well in his bold attempts to instil new life in the art of motion, to discover new forms and new beauties. One cannot think of Fokin's Ballets without Pavlova : she is the only one whose name is associated with the new undertaking, with the prophetic power, a live source of hitherto unrevealed beauty, which has already triumphed at Paris.

Photo Van Riel.

PAVLOVA
in the " Bacchanal "

" By virtue of her sublime enthusiasm and beauty, Pavlova has led us to believe in the vitality and soul of that art, hardly explored as yet, and whose field lies in the future. For a long time our best hopes have been placed in her; and it is around her that the impetus towards dancing, which seem to spread so fast and far, is taking shape. "

We have already quoted the views of Russian critics such as S. Andreevsky, S. Belaief, Levinson, A. Plestsheef, and others.

There is as much to cull from the field of French criticism. Louis

Laloy, Alfred Bruneau, Nozière, Sébastien Voirol (to name only these few) have written on her dancing.

To the excerpts quoted in previous chapter let us add a few characteristic utterances.

In an article entitled '' Terpsichora Reborn'', M. Sébastien Voirol writes :

'' Anna Pavlova creates the most exquisite emotions, primarily by virtue of the dazzling radiance of a quality rarely met with under similar circumstances : intelligence. In her creation *The Swan's Death*, the intelligence which she evinces comes straight from the heart. For us, moreover, the soulful quality of her gestures and movements bears the very hall-mark of that most elusive of things, genius.

'' For that reason alone, and solely through the rhythm of her attitudes, which reaches so far beyond the rhythm of music, she creates for us art under a form impossible to compare with anything given us by Phidias or da Vinci.

'' After having expressed her well-weighed admiration for Fokin and Isadora Duncan, and referred to the production of *Eunice,* which marks the dawn of the Renaissance of dancing in Russia, she uttered these simple words : '' without the heart there can be no genuine expression, no genuine art even in dancing ''.

'' Here is indeed an eternal truth, but a truth often overlooked at the present time. The heart — that is, sensitiveness at its keenest, fervid comprehension, all-conquering enthusiasm, soul and body working in perfect harmony; that is, the live flame without which no work of art can move nor conquer the human mind. And that gift of hers consigns the mere craft of the Ballerina to oblivion: we no longer see ought but the pure miracle evoked ''.

In 1920, M. Raymond Charpentier wrote in *Comœdia :*

'' As a classical dancer, Anna Pavlova is an apex, a *non plus ultra*. That seems to be an admitted fact, which none could hope successfully to question. Besides, I do not think that anybody wishes to question it.

'' Upon this mere matter of technique, agreement should in any case be reached easily. For Pavlova's virtuosity greatly exceeds what had hitherto been considered as perfection. Her feet, trained to the utmost possible limit, simply play with technical difficulties. But for a Ballerina such as she, the feet are a mere detail, a kind of live support and nothing more. Of far greater significance is the full co-operation of her whole physical being. The harmony of her gestures is marred by no deficiency and no discord. An undulation of her shoulders, a trill of her waist, are completed by the curvation of her neck and arms, lithe as bamboo stems undulating under the breeze. Not a muscle in her body which perfect adaptability and training does not enable to participate in the action, to co-operate in the expression of a feeling, an image, an idea, a symbol. A case in point is her remarkable interpretation of *The Swan's Death*, now justly famous, and indeed never to be forgotten. She is wonderfully supple, imponderable at times. Even gravitation seems at times to forego its rights when she dances. She dances as the dove flies, as the flower blooms, giving us something immateriate, something similar to what we conceive the play of extra-terrestrial forces to be.

" Anna Pavlova is first and last an artist.

" Otherwise, how could she produce *ensembles* such as that of the Blue Danube Waltz, as delightful in their choregraphic arrangement as in their disposition and scheme of lights and colours?

" She brings us things to admire in countless profusion. Her programme comprises, besides separate dance-numbers, Adolphe Adam's *Giselle,* whose scenario is by Henri Saint-Georges and Theophile Gautier. I am no great admirer of Adam's old-fashioned music; but I must acknowledge that *Giselle* is a perfectly acceptable and suitable work. And Pavlova's success in it was unanimous. That may show that so long as she will devote her peerless talent to real music, she will be hailed by all as the Queen of Dance, and reign unchallenged ".

Here is another opinion, supplied by M. René Jean (in *Comœdia,* 1920).

" Lithe, slender, full of life and glow, Pavlova, as soon as she starts to move, seems about to embrace the whole world, and enclose the infinite within the circle of her arms. All of her is rhythm and harmony. Her person is instinct with such a wealth of vitality, that her every gesture spreads beyond reality, and seems to borrow the quality of eternity. She possesses the genius of Dance, a genius which exalts the human body, transfigures and idealises it, magnifies it reverently, and achieves a style so noble as to impress us with the feeling of absolute perfection. At the very moment when we are the most deeply moved, we deplore that the movements which impress us with so rare an emotion should be so transient.

" Her regular features, slender and delicate, and, above the beautifully modelled cheek-bones, the glowing deep eyes wrapt in fervid contemplation, lend themselves to the greatest variety of suggestions.

She is the living sister of yon dancers who, standing forth from a fragment of marble in the British Museum, recall to our mind the recondite beauty of the old Egyptian world; she is a nymph in that train of Aphrodite's pageant inscribed on the surface of the Greek Vase in our own Louvre; she is one of the Maenads on that Greek marble which is the pride of the Uffizi at Florence. But, above all things, she is one of the dancing priestesses of Corneto, which the Etrurians had enclosed in the Triclinio tomb, where they were to delight with their beauty, time out of mind, the dead one graced with their company.

" For like those priestesses, Pavlova, the aerial Sylph, carries the art of movement to its supreme level. The whole of her body takes part in every shade of expression. Her hands are eloquent as the voice of a Tribune or, rather, the oration of a Priest whose words bring comfort. For it is their religiosity that constitutes the greatness of the dancing figures bequeathed to us by the old world. Nothing in their attitudes and movements is profane, or low, or perverse : sacerdotal gravity is impressed upon their features and the whole of their bodies. Even the Bacchants, in their frenzy, devote themselves to a rite whose spirit carries them far beyond the visible world. And religiosity is a feature of Pavlova's deep, concentrated love for her art : the fervid gift she has made to dancing of her whole life and mind is in a way the outcome of a sacerdotal vocation.

" But although what she expresses is essentially herself, through the creation of attitudes and gestures inspired solely by her own sensitiveness, by her emotions as a human being under the spell of music, Pavlova is acquainted with the whole range of dances ancient and recent. Italian fantasy and French grace are things no less familiar to her than Eastern gravity and Slavonic mysticism. She knows all our painters, and has studied those who sought inspiration in the world of dancing. In her appreciation of them she shows an undeniable sense of logic. Consider, for instance, her opinion on Degas, whom she does not like because " he has delineated attitudes and not movements ". There we have, in concise form, a full profession of aesthetic faith : for indeed Pavlova's movements create the most perfect expressions in plastic form which a painter or sculptor might dream of. "

From an impressive article by Madame Florian Delhorde, entitled " A Farewell to Pavlova ", we shall content ourselves with quoting the following lines :

" Pavlova is the very soul of Dance. Upon the stage, she appears transfigured, she no longer belongs to herself. She is not the woman

she was a while before, a woman like all those which surround her.
The others are flesh and blood, but in her there is something immat-
erial. When she represents the soul of Giselle in the graveyard, she
ceases to be terrestrial, she becomes aerial. While her dancing-
partner raises her up into the air, life seems to forsake her. She all
but vanishes from our sight. Her gestures float away, vibrate further
and further, like sounds dying in the distance. She is Rhythm made
visible. The whole of her vibrates, she is a tremendous unity. Her
person is a high-power instrument, and at the same time something
highly elusive. There is infinite fragility in her legs so full of wit,
in her feet so full of style. She is imponderable, and yet has muscles
of steel. When she takess a jump, you do not see her gather momentum to rise from the ground; you would think her attracted skywards,
as a puppet might be by a wire. Thus, in Andersen's tale, the little
paper dancing-girl floats across the room, carried by a gust of wind.
She commands a faultless technique, and yields to emotion unreservedly.

" She inspires us with love for Russia, and teaches us to appreciate perfection ".

Let us end with a quotation from a critic who preferred to remain
anonymous, and who speaks as follows, in *Le Journal du Peuple,* of
Pavlova and her art :

" Dancing is carried out to music. Could it not be likewise
carried out to the sound of beautiful verses? When, under the minis-
trations of Anna Pavlova, Dance reigns supreme, it is in harmony
with the very rhythms which both musicians and poets sing to.
Dance is a moving form of poetry; a form which inspires similar
passions, and perhaps a richer variety of dreams. One can easily
realise how it came to pass that one day Théophile Gautier, yielding
to his fancy, should have conceived the Ballet *Giselle* and joined
forces with the composer Adolphe Adam. For he had been prompted
by the vision of the poem which later materialised on the stage, to
the sound of music, by virtue of a dancer's achievements. And yet, it
was not given to him to see Pavlova. Even we, who had applauded
her masterful renderings of separate dance-numbers, could never
have conceived anything so splendid as the revelation of her in that
part.

" Everybody knows how full of grace she is, how supple and
lithe; everybody has admired the pure beauty of her gestures and the
unerring accuracy of her steps. We ourselves have more than once
described her talent as worthy of the epithet sublime. We have

PAVLOVA Dancing

PAVLOVA Dancing

spoken of the surpassing eloquence of her rendering of *The Swan's Death*. Eloquence, we see, is not the privilege of the spoken word, which charms, but once uttered sinks into oblivion.

" With *Giselle* her choregraphic genius finds a new, equally powerful expression. Sensuousness, dexterity, virtuosity are discarded in favour of new means, which express, in singularly accurate and forcible wise, all that the poet had dreamt for his heroine. It is no longer mere dancing, it is dancing coupled with something infinitely greater. What we see is a tragedy, whose serene beauty would equal that of one by Racine if only Adam's music was not so strikingly inferior. Our imagination and sensitiveness are kindled by the sight of that interpreter who, no longer a dancer, but a genuine human being, gives the whole of herself in her woebegone miming, her pregnant, spirited gestures, expressive, impassioned, doleful. Her death is a lovely poem which moves our very soul to tears.

" The resurrection in another world, the egress from the tomb, and all the childish allegorical stuff that follows become splendid when interpreted by her. She is indeed, in that part, a creature from regions unearthly ".

Herr Oskar Bie, the well-known autor of a standard book entitled *Dance*, has devoted in that work the following lines to Pavlova :

" A special interest (I might say, an organic interest) which I took in dancing led me to write a bulky volume on that subject; for I had a dim foreboding that our time would bring with it a renaissance of that art.

" I had just finished my book when I became acquainted with Pavlova. My acquaintanceship with her had twofold results, partly good, partly bad. They were bad insofar as I realised that, had I met Pavlova sooner, I should have understood through her, far better than it was possible to learn in any other wise, what Dance was. But after this first impression came the feeling, most definite, that I had not devoted my labour to a subject for which there was no future ".

Further, reverting to Pavlova :

" The whole of her individuality, the whole of her art, so highly original, all the features which caracterise her, are in intimate connection with the idiosyncrasies of to-day's Russia. The Russians are coming to the arts very belatedly. For that very reason, they are spared the burden of many a grave error, and they have the advantage of being able to study old forms of art in the light of modern conceptions. And the very psychological idiosyncrasies of their race have resulted in particularly striking conceptions of that kind.

" We have seen it in Russian opera, we see it now in dancing. In the time-honoured scheme of lyric tragedy, Tchaïkowsky introduced a feeling far deeper than any of his predecessors had done.   The

Photo Matzene.

PAVLOVA
IN " LA FÉE DES POUPÉES "

operas of Glinka bear the mark of revolutionary tendencies which greatly outrun the usual scheme of works of that pattern.   Dargomyjsky and Mussorgsky were greater innovators that Debussy is.

" As a consequence of that conflict between form and substance, Russia suffers, but progresses.   And nowhere are the struggle and contrast to be seen so thorough, and followed with so beautiful and harmonious results, as in Pavlova's dances.

" She is a modern artist who performs antiquated steps, fully equipped as regards technique, yet always in quest of the spirit.   Ingeniously, unconsciously, she translates the subtlest elements which are to be disengaged from them ".

Another German art-critic, Herr Max Osborne, writes :

" Berlin will never forget that night at the Kroll-Theater when for the first time we yielded to the spell of the Russian dancers. It was an almost terrifying experience. Nothing could have been more impressive than the sudden materialisation of dreams and hopes which were thought to exceed the boundaries of the possible. It seemed as though a miracle had brought that imposing array of artists before us. And all paid spontaneous homage to the majestic figure of that being instinct with youth and sweetness who was fluttering in their midst, a queenly presence inded : Anna Pavlova ".

The *Coventry Times* (January 1912) writes :

" The celebrated Russian dancer Anna Pavlova, whose reputation is world-wide, and who has been the craze of London, Paris, Berlin and other continental cities, has appeared on the stage of the Theatre Royal, Conventry.

" To describe her dances is no easy task. One must see her in order fully to realise how exquisite and marvellous her art is. Her interpretations are perfection, and constitute as many delightful poems of motion ".

Here are a few remarks which appeared in *The Graphic* (May 1912):

" Dancing is a simple thing, yet one difficult to describe or define with any degree of accuracy. In my opinion, the best critics would be embarrassed if they were asked to supply a full description of Pavlova's art...

" I admired her the other night on the stage, resplendent in a halo of rose-petals. I felt almost carried away upon the wings of a wonderful morning breeze. I was following the flight of an iridescent cloud floating away in the glory of dawn. I saw in Pavlova's art the splendour of a soul born before my eyes, and rejoiced exceedingly ".

La Noche de la Habana (March 1915) devotes to Pavlova an article from which we quote the following interesting passages :

" At the basis of all the pictures provided by Pavlova's dances we find the worship of line and proportion, the fundamental condition of all things are she conceives them. All motions and evolutions of her body proceed in accordance with an order, a system whose principal element is line — a principle by the application of which she is able to express anything, from the most primitive forms of feeling to the most complex action.

" There is nothing novel in that method : it was known in times long past. But Pavlova's merit is to have substituted adequate, scientific notions to the hitherto prevailing empiricism. Her art is founded on the study of artistic anatomy : that is, on anatomical studies pursued with an artistic objet in view.

" It was possible for so powerful a mind as Pavlova's to succeed in this difficult task. And one can well realise how colossal an amount of labour she has had to perform in order thoroughly to acquaint herself with the muscular system, so as to acquire the capacity to conceive images in the form under which she offers them to her audiences : i. e., under the twofold aspect of line and expression.

" Yet another point has to be considered. The images which she creates are not copied from nature : they are the splendid fruit of her own imagination. Even her passions bear the imprint of a certain austerity, which stiffens her features and represses the outbursts of certain over-strong emotions. Ancient art has certainly influenced Pavlova : for one discovers classical features in every one of her dances. All that might be soft or lascivious yields to the sway of pure line ; the impetus of the soul conquers the instinct of the senses ".

" Nothing could equal my feeling of delight " Laura G. de Zayas-Bazan wrote in *La Prensa* in 1915. " Words cannot express the artistic emotion which overcame me during the marvellous spectacle afforded by that peerless artist, Anna Pavlova.

" I should never have thought that rythms of motion and plastic perfection could affect me so deeply, penetrating my soul to the very inmost, and generating the painful feeling which, under the stress of emotion, the overwrought nerves transmit to the very surface of the flesh. I felt myself vibrating like a harp !

" The Swan's Dance, admirably interpreted in the undulations of her beautiful body, and throughout which one felt the very pulse of genius, was for me a poem instinct with sublimity and pathos, genuine and wonderful in its vitality.

" And what can I say of the *Autumn Bacchanal ?* It is so full of glow, of spirit, so ardent in the sway of its passion, so dignified in its sheer beauty, so graceful, so Olympian when the famous artist and her partner dance it in its true character of a Pagan song of love !

" One can hardly believe that she is the same woman who, a moment before, was impersonating the Swan, the chaste bird whose wings flutter poetically in the throes of death, on the bank of the deep lake surrounded by willows and cypress-trees ".

In her account of an interview with Pavlova, the same writer confesses that she had never felt so deeply impressed and moved.

" Those who meet Pavlova for the first time " she says " seem to lose all power of speech. They feel they are in the presence of a

PAVLOVA
A sketch by Gir

superior being. A mysterious intellectual force emanates from her person ''.

Here is a recent article from the pen of Nozière.

'' Anna Pavlova is a miracle of balance and grace. When she stands on the tip of one foot, she is altogether aerial. You would hardly wonder if you saw her take her flight. Her rendering of Tchaïkovsky's *Snowflakes* revives the whole classical art of dancing. It is a sequence of perfect visions — in which Alexandre Volinine is entirely worthy of his great partner. It is thus, probably, that the best artists would dance before king Louis XIV, and in the XVIIth century.

'' As for Sibelius's *Valse Triste,* it enables Pavlova and Volinine to conjure a vision of the milder charm of romanticism. The *Syrian Dance,* to Saint-Saëns's music, recalls the splendour and the Eastern brutality of *Sheherazade.* The elegance of a Minuet, the picturesqueness of a Flower-Dance, ensured further triumphs for Pavlova. But it is with her interpretation of '' the Swan's Death '' that she roused the audience to enthusiasm. This dance contains things that quiver like wings, and are as pellucid as the purest water. It is altogether admirable ''.

PAVLOVA
A sketch by Gir

M. Louis Schneider writes with reference to Pavlova's last performances in Paris :

" For the benefit of the " Œuvre des orphelins de Guerre Français et Russes " presided by the Duchesse d'Uzès, the famous dancer Anna Pavlova with her company has given, at the Trocadéro, the first of a new series of performances. It was with unalloyed pleasure that all returned to see the peerless Russian artist in a new set of dances and scenes. For the main characteristic of Pavlova is that she does not content herself with being a wonderful virtuoso : she gives us thoughtful acting, illuminated with the countless flashes of things imagined with infinite charm and wit, and accomplished with instinctive, matchless grace. Every time Pavlova appeared, she was greeted with endless applause, whether she danced with her altogether worthy partner Volinin a classical Pas de Deux, or alone Tchaïkovsky's *Californian Poppy* — and how delighfully, at the end of that dance, she translates in her movements the closing of the petals!

In the second part of the evening, she danced with infinite briskness an alert Minuet by Massenet, and after that *The Swan's Death* by Saint-Saëns, in which she causes so tragic a thrill to run through her audience at the moment when she shows us the death of the bird beloved by Jupiter. An enthusiastic public cheered her and encored without end ".

M. André Cœuroy writes :

" Wereas Isadora Duncan strives to delight the ear as well as the eye, by selecting for her dances good music — not always altogether suitable for her purposes — Anna Pavlova, in this period which has brought so strange an upheaval in all intellectual values, has understood that what was expected by us was dance to music, and not music danced.

" Her dancing and attitudes are never the slaves of music, but assert the absolute power of her inexhaustible imagination. Pavlova, the splendid virtuoso of that movement which shifts the lines but never breaks them, was greeted last night, after the public rehearsal of the spectacles organised by the Théâtre Russe de Paris in favour of Russian and French war orphans, with an enthusiasm of which a fair and ample share went to the artists who appear with her ".

The composer Reynaldo Hahn writes, with reference to her performances of *La Péri* :

" *La Péri* is one of the very finest things in modern instrumental music. One could imagine nothing richer, brighter, more pellucid, more refined than the scoring with which Mr Paul Dukas has graced

PAVLOVA and VOLININ
in the " Bacchanal "
Statue by Malvina Hoffman

his Dance-Poem. The Persian miniaturists have never done anything more artistic, more subtle, more intense and delicate in hues.

" Pavlova, who appears in the title-part under an aspect new to
us, carries into her miming that very poetry which is one of the most
delightful features in her dancing. And her partner Stowitz, in a
sumptuous, cleverly contrived garb — quality making up for scant-
iness — is elegant and expressive in the part of the Prince ".

M. Antoine Banès writes in the *Figaro* (1921).

" 'No, Sir! Anna Pavlova is no dancer: she is a direct emanation
from Paradise!' Thus did one of the most peacefully-inclined men
I know speak to me the other day, with challenging virulence.   His

enthusiasm brought a smile upon my lips, and made me think that he himself must be " an emanation " of the southern climes where hyperbole flourishes, despite his brazen assertion that he did not hail from yon regions of the Earthly Paradise. But since the wonderful evening I spent yesterday at the Trocadéro, I have given up my scepticism; and I acknowledge that my excitable friend was altogether in the right.

" I do not remember having ever seen anything more perfect in quality, more comprehensive that the selection of dances contributed by Pavlova. I did not believe it possible that we could watch dances three hours running, without intermission or constrast, and not experience some degree of weariness.

" Pavlova and her admirable company have brought us convincing proof to the contrary, and made us realise a thing which I doubted : viz, that choregraphy is capable of expressing the utmost variety of feelings down to their most subtle shades. Could it be possible to interpret with greater intensity of emotion the Valse Triste, in which the poet and his Muse evoke so suavely and rhythmically the spell of the mysterious night of October or May? Could anything be more witty, more beautifully finished than those evolutions, sentimental or bellicose, performed by *The Little Tin Soldiers?* Could there exist a *Brigand* more truculent thant M. Stowitz in his superb impersonation of that part? Would any *Pierrot* dream of competing with the wonderful M. Volinin? Is there an artist who, after Anna Pavlova, would be so rash as to interpret the *Swan's Death?*

" Indeed, nothing could be more touching, more deeply thrilling that the last named scene, with the slow silent agony which moves us to the quick, better than any words could, by virtue of its simple pathetic poetry. And words fail to translate the charm of the *Californian Poppy* whose petals, a moment open, gently close like a casket of purple over the flower which yields to the withering rays of the sun.

" What chiefly attracts and charms us in Anna Pavlova and her companions is the intelligent, well-weighed simplicity of their talent. There is no smack of the laboured or the artificial in the wonderful effects which they achieve, without ever sacrificing to mere effect their choregraphic science nor their sense of dramatic fitness.

" Of the eighteen numbers wich they provided, there is no single one which calls for the slightest criticism. They are, for the most part, produced by Ivan Clustin; and all are unimpeachably carried out. The delightful music, clear and perspicuous, which accompanies them, the costumes, sober yet beautiful in hues and cleverly varied, add to the undefinable charm of the spectacle. This show is a dream of tender sweetness and pure beauty, which no single art-lover should fail to see forthwith. It is indeed an emanation from the paradise of art. We are to have five of those delightful performances, which should be eagerly followed, not only for their sheer magnificence, but because they are given with a most praiseworthy object : to the benefit of the Anna Pavlova Foundation in Paris for the Russian refugee children and the French war-widows and orphans. They are organised under the patronage of Madame Alexandre Millerand and the Duchesse d'Uzès ".

In the *Revue de l'Epoque* (1921) has appeared an interesting and curious article by Sébastien Voirol, describing the great artist at her private work — that is, under an aspect which the public at large is unacquainted with. It is entitled " Anna Pavlova rehearsing ".

" ' Here she is, she who is named Sigeh, Ennoia, Barbelo, Prounikos! Did you not know it was she? ' I intimated by a shake of my head that I had no use for trivial and otherwise superfluous words. I found the speaker intolerable in his absent-mindedness. Perhaps he thought that the rehearsal had started in too lackadaisical and uninteresting fashion.

" To begin with, an unknown violonist had appeared from nowhere and played Saint-Saëns' *Havanaise* to an organ accompaniment, while in another corner, by the piano, Hilda Butsova was practising her exercises at the bars. After that, a group of Japanese sailors had come to visit the hall — which offers very little interest except when one is privileged to witness Anna Pavlova rehearsing. Apart from that, my friend was surrounded by other spectators, many of whom were unknown to him.

" M. Paul Dukas, the composer of *La Péri,* was quietly conferring with M. Jacques Rouché. René Piot, the artist who painted the scenery for that work, was explaining, with a wealth of vehement gesticulation, some important point of aesthetics to the conductor, M. Philippe Gaubert. Ivan Clustin, the Ballet-master, was issuing brief instructions in a low voice.

" Our eyes were focussed upon the stage, upon which the Dance-Poem, that most beautiful of poems, was about to be revealed to us for the first time.

" But the Peri, opening her eyes, clapped her hands once and cried aloud,

" For it was impossible for her to rise towards the Light of Ormuzd.

" And meanwhile Iskender, looking into her face, admired her features, which were more lovely than even those of Gurdafferid.

" And he yearned for her within his heart.

" Thus did the Peri know the thoughts which were in the King's mind.

" For the Lotus in Iskender's right hand grew red, and became like to the face of Desire.

" And therefore she, the Servant of the Pure, realised that yon Flower of Life was not intended for her.

" And in order to grasp it, she rushed forward, as swift as the bee.

" Then the Invincible Lord drew the Lotus out of her reach, and was torn between his thirst for immortality and the delight before his eyes.

" But the Peri started to dance the Dance of the Peris,

" Coming nearer and nearer to Iskender, until her face touched his;

" So that at last, he returned the Flower to her willingly.

" Then did the Lotus become like to snow and gold, like to the peak of Elbruz in the glow of the setting sun.

" And the Peris's form seemed to melt in the radiance shed by the Flower.   Soon nothing of her person remain visible except a hand, raising towards heaven the Flower of Flame, and slowly lost to sight as it floated into the Upper Regions.

" Iskender saw her vanish;

" And understood that thus he was to know that his own end was near.

" And he felt the shadow encircling him ".

" While the orchestra strikes the first bars, Pavlova takes off the high tiara she was wearing.   Her costume is that of the Perfect Fairy, according to the Asiatic notion.   It is designed by her partner Hugo Stowitz, a young artist from North America.   She exhales an atmosphere of religion and fervour.   Gradually, she begins to move and expresses animation.   Her hair are loosened and fall in black waves over her shoulders, adorning her even more becomingly, and expressing in tangible form, so to speak, something of that most unaccountable glow wich emanates from all her being, of that most impressive of all the powers which the gods have bestowed upon our world.

" From the auditorium a friendly voice, interpreting the composer's views, warns the accompanist : *Slishkom Skoro* (too fast).

" Then our Peri makes for the Upper Regions (which to-day are situated behind the unpretentious green hangings decorating the stage of the Trocadero) to take there a well-earned rest. My friend — by name Ulric Nestvedt — remains a while wrapt in thought, then begins to display ill-temper.

" I was reading the other day in *Comœdia* " he said, " that " Taglioni would have envied her aerial grace ", and that " she is the very picture of what Fanny Elssler must have been ". Such comparisons are most irritating. Are our critics incapable of feeling? Do they not realise that from the moment when this woman appears, even before she dances, we confront a genius whose sense of art and capacity for seduction are beyond compare, and unlike anything we have ever seen? That she is and will remain unique?

— But, I retorted, it is a point of dogma that one cannot be considered intelligent unless one is endowed with some degree of scepticism.

— Yet, when you have to listen to arguments founded upon the very reverse of what dogma implies, and common sense calls for, even you would feel bewildered.

— I shall never forgive, I interposed, that very clever writer G. de la Fouchardière for having dared to compare Anna Pavlova with a bird of the genus flamingo who would be endowed with a surpassing capacity for acrobatic virtuosity ".

" But Nada Quiero, suddenly taking a hand in the conversation, replied :

" All that is nothing. Have you ever heard René Doumic discourse of Flaubert? It is exactly the same thing, and does not matter in the least. What exasperates me is to find an author as full of excellent intentions as for instance M. Nozière write that " she evinces a delicate sensitiveness ". It is he indeed who evinces the " delicate sensitiveness " in stereotyped form when he ventures to speak of her whom M. Louis Laloy has described as " the angel of dance " in terms which he might apply to any promising young debutant ".

" Nada Quiero is right — right as usual, and I told her as much.

— Indeed, I said, nobody of us has succeeded in suitably describing all that Anna Pavlova can express in one gesture, whether spiritual and hinting of a world afar, or languid and graceful, with that touch of melancholy which belongs to a fleeting thought whose sudden appearance is enough to fill our soul for the brief duration of our own " evermore ".

" I had reckoned without the retentiveness of Nada Quiero's extraordinary memory.

— But some one has described all that, and most adequately.

PAVLOVA
Statuette by Troubetzkoy

Remember those two sentences by Gaston de Pawlowski : " Her peerless talent seems to include all forms of art-expression which have cropped up in any period. To move the heart to tears with mere simulacra of life is easy : but to draw tears from the utmost depths of the soul because one has succeeded in arousing that prototype of Beauty which lurks in those depths, that is a privilege almost divine ".

" But after her brief rest, the Peri reappears on the stage. The pianist goes on with the fluid and sparkling music — which Nada Quiero considers slightly cold — and again we are carried into the very heart of the poem. Iskender roves through Iran, in quest of the flower of immortality. He discovers the Peri asleep, and ravishes the beautiful Lotos. We are merged in an ocean of delight.

" When the rehearsal is ended, Nada Quiero, who dislikes the conventional attitudes, greetings, compliments, and small-talk which are *de rigueur* at the close of those social functions, ask us whether it is possible to slink out without crossing the stage, which the guests are now crowding. She vanishes, Ulric Nestvedt in her wake.

" The officially invited guests follow.

" For a while, I remain on the stage, alone but for the company of Poppy, the good little Boston terrier who, pending the reapparance of his mistress, is actively worrying a bit of wood. Soon Volinin appears, and after him Goldschmann, who is to conduct the orchestra. He sits down in front of the piano and begins to play Rubinstein's *Valse Caprice*.

" But all of a sudden, the shadow which had fallen upon Iskender seems to lift. Kindly, uplifting light seems to liven the dull, dusty flooring, the walls, and the lifeless organ. Pavlova has reappeared, radiant in her everyday clothes : black skirt, white blouse and foot-wear, but hatless. She has now to explain to the young conductor the *tempi* which he will have to take. And again she begins to dance. But it is no longer the dance of the Peris. It is a form of art alto-gether new to us plain human beings. With slight gestures of the arms, hardly perceptible motions of the bust and torso, she dances, she seems to take her flight, to overcome every law of gravity, while the soles of her shoes remain firmly set upon the floor. It is from her very soul that the rhythms dictated by her are emanating.

" With a glance, she begs me to be patient until the end of the necessary process of adjustment.

" But could I be impatient? The next time I see Ulric Nest-vedt, I shall peremptorily prove to him that there is no such thing as impatience ".

CONCLUSION

 ET a few words suffice by way of conclusion to this monograph devoted to the greatest dancer of this century.

I do no tknow whether I have succeeded in emphasising the various merits and aspects of her talent, which distinguish her so strikingly from all other priestesses of the choregraphic art. The idiosyncrasies of her nature as an artist, the zeal with which she has pursued the education of both her body and her mind, and — last but not least — the extraordinary willpower which governs her frail being, are the chief causes of her successes. As soon as she appears, her audience falls under her sway. By virtue of which charms does she thus acquire her wonderful power over the motley, fickle public of the theatre? Which mysterious agency is it that enables her to hold all spectators thus spell-bound?

I think that a possible explanation to this mystery of psychology is to be found in the following passage from Georges Clemenceau's *Le Voile du Bonheur* :

" Chinese tradition says as to the science of governement, that he alone who understands music is capable of governing — and this applies with even more truth as regards music combined with dancing ". It is said in the Book of Rites that from a nation's dances you can judge its customs. The reason is that *dancing is nothing other than a harmonious compendium of the movements of life*. Hence its importance ".

Adopting that point of view, we shall have no difficulty in acknowledging the invaluable services rendered by Pavlova to the cause of Russian art. Her untiring, ungrudging activities, carried out in many different parts of the world, have been the boldest, most energetic, most eloquent propaganda in favour of her country's art. As Mussorgsky in his music and Shaliapin in his singing, she has revealed in her dancing the true soul of the Russian people.

But how did it come to pass that Pavlova, who is a classic *par excellence*, should have pursued so triumphant a career precisely at a time infatuated with modernity and the up-to date at all costs, which is already considering cubism as a back-number, and seems to make headway towards some goal, not yet distinctly perceptible, but not far distant perhaps from dadaism; at a time when, as M. Georges Masson puts it, " the word, pleasant, has become fraught with obloquy; and to say of a writer that his style is pleasant is equivalent to casting an aspersion on that style? "

We live at a time singularly rich in complications from the psychological point of view. On one hand, we can notice a leaning towards that modern art which M. Georges Masson calls " unpleasant art "; on the other hand, a no less powerful current carries us back towards the past, towards ancient forms. Never did any time evince more keen an appreciation of works belonging to long-past periods than our time does.

But the contradiction, although very striking, is only on the surface. All things considered, " old " and " new " are but relative values; and cubism as well as classical choregraphy may become threadbare. Indeed, it is a fact that at the very moment when we began to feel weary of such things as *Parades*, we turned to *Giselle* with refreshed interest.

Let us remember, with reference to the above remark, how the Old Believers of Russia welcomed Peter the Great's ultra-modernist reforms. " The innovation you introduce " they said " have something in them which belongs to the old order ". A chart of the variations of art would greatly resemble a weather chart. Currents alter

PAVLOVA
IN "THE SWAN'S DEATH"
STATUETTE BY ROSALÈS

their direction, meet, mingle, split, diverge; now they are at cross-purposes, now they co-operate.

In art, forms are eternally changing, forms are ever cropping up and vanishing. " All is transient. Truth alone perishes not ", says the song in one of Andersen's tales. In art, the Truth which abides is Talent. Genuine talent is able to create new values out of anti-quated materials, without having to reckon with passing fashions. And that is the reason why Pavlova shines with equal brilliancy in *Giselle*, that work of the past, or in *La Péri*, which is of our own time. The vitality of great talents is such, that they outshine and transform all that surrounds them. That is why the democratic republics of old Greece ostracised them. But our time realises that talent is one of the finest things in the world, a thing which brings to us the spirit from above, and turns all that it touches into gold. Therefore, our time need never investigate whether a work of art is old or new.

THE END

ANNA PAVLOVA'S REPERTORY

⛆

AT THE PETROGRAD
THEATRE MARIE

I. — PARTS AND DANCES

BALLETS	CHARACTERS AND DANCES	COMPOSERS
Pharao's Daughter	Pas de trois *(In the Act of the « Caryatides »)*	PUGNI
Marcobombe	Pas de trois	PUGNI
Harlequinade	Pas de quatre *(With Michel Fokine)*	DRIGO
La Fée des Poupées	The Spanish Doll	BAYER
Casse-Noisette	La Valse d'or	TCHAIKOVSKY
La Source	L'Éphéméride	MINKUS-DELIBES
Pharao's Daughter	Pas d'action	PUGNI
Esméralda	Fleur de Lys's friend	PUGNI
Blue Beard	Sister Anna	CHENK
Raymonda	Raymonda's friend Panadéros	GLAZOUNOF
Paquita	Pas de trois	DELDEVEZ
Camargo	La Neige *(Variation)*	PUGNI
La Bayadère	Pas de trois	MINKUS

BALLETS	PARTS AND DANCES	COMPOSERS
	La fée Candide	
The Sleeping Beauty	La princesse Florine	TCHAIKOWSKY
	The Fairy of the Lilacs	
King Candaulus	Pas de Diane	PUGNI
Koniok Gorbounok (*The Hobby-Horse*)	Dance of the Ural Cossacks	PUGNI
Fiametta	The page	PUGNI
Coppélia	Svanilde's friend	DELIBES
Don Quichotte	Juanita, seller of fans	MINKUS
The Magic Mirror	The princess	KORESTCHENKO
The four Seasons	Autumn (*Bacchanal*)	GLAZOUNOF

II. — BALLETS

BALLETS	PARTS AND DANCES	COMPOSERS
The Vine	The Bacchant	A. RUBINSTEIN
The Magic Flute	Lisette	DRIGO
Flora's Awakening	Flora	DRIGO
The Enchanted Forest	The Maiden	DRIGO
Eunice	Eunice	STCHERBATCHEF
Chopiniana	The Sylph	CHOPIN
Nuits d'Egypte	Véronique	ARENSKY
Pavillon d'Armide	Armide	TCHEREPNIN
The Naïad and the Fisherman	The Naïad	PUGNI
Paquita	Paquita	DELDEVEZ
Giselle	Giselle	ADAM
La Bayadère	Nicaea	MINKUS
Pharao's Daughter	Aspicchia	PUGNI
King Candaulus	Likia	PUGNI
The Sleeping Beauty	Princess Aurora	TCHAIKOVSKY
Don Quichotte	Kitri	MINKUS
The Corsair	Médora	ADAM ET PUGNI

III. — OPERAS

BALLETS	PARTS AND DANCES	COMPOSERS
Rousslan and Ludmila	Lesghinka	GLINKA
A Life for the Tsar	Mazurka	GLINKA
Carmen	Olé	BIZET
The Demon	Lesghinka	A. RUBINSTEIN

EUROPE AND AMERICA

I. — BALLETS

BALLETS	PARTS AND DANCES	COMPOSERS
Harlequinade	Colombine	DRIGO
Paquita	Paquita	DELDEVEZ
Giselle	Giselle	ADAM
La Fille mal gardée	Lise	HÉROLD
Le Lac des Cygnes	Odette-Odylle	TCHAIKOVSKY
Coppélia	Svanilde	DELIBES
Amarilla	Amarilla, the Gipsy	PUGNI
Les Préludes	The Happy Shadow	LISZT
The Seven Daughters of the King	Crystal-Clear-Spring	SPENDIAROF
Flora's Awakening	Flora	DRIGO
The Magic Flute	Lise	DRIGO
Nuits Arabes	Fatima	ARENDS
La Halte de Cavalerie	Thérèse	ARMSHEIMER
L'Orient (Une Nuit sur le Mont Chauve)	The Houri	MOUSSORGSKY
Invitation à la Valse	The Young Girl	WEBER
La Fée des Poupées	The Fairy	BAYER
Chopiniana	The Sylph	CHOPIN
Raymonda	Raymonda	GLAZOUNOF
The Sleeping Beauty	Princesse Aurora	TCHAIKOVSKY
The Snowflake (Casse-Noisette)	Le Flocon	TCHAIKOVSKY
Les Chèvres-pieds	La Faunesse	SATZ
La Péri	La Péri	P. DUKAS
Ballet Égyptien	The Egyptian	LUIGINI
Feuilles d'Automne	The Chysanthemum	CHOPIN
Les Trois Pantins de Bois	The Little Girl	M. M. LÉVY
Schubertiana	The Queen of Dryades	SCHUBERT
Les Noces Polonaises (Airs populaires polonais)	The Fiancée	SCHUBERT
Dyonisos	The Priestess	TCHEREPNIN
Ultimo Canto	La jeune fiancée	MAURAGE
Black and White	The Mischievous Pupil	CHAMINADE

II. — OPERAS

Thaïs	Thaïs	MASSENET
Faust (Valpurgis' Night)	Helen	GOUNOD
Orphée	The Shadow	GLUCK
Mephistofele	The Nymph	BOÏTO
Moïse	The Slave	DONIZETTI
Carmen	Spanish dances	BIZET
Romeo and Juliette	The Queen of Springtide	GOUNOD
Guarani (Brasilian Opera)	The Indian woman	GOMEZ

III. — DIVERTISSEMENTS

BALLETS	COMPOSERS
The Swan	SAINT-SAËNS
The Dragon Fly	KREISLER
The Butterfly	DRIGO
Californian Poppy	TCHAIKOVSKY
The Night	A. RUBINSTEIN
The Dying Rose	DRIGO
Rondino	KREISLER
La Danse	KREISLER
Syrian Dance (Samson and Dalila)	SAINT-SAËNS
Bacchanal	GLAZOUNOF
Mexican Dances (Folktunes)	
Gavotte Pavlova	LINKE
Valse triste	SIBELIUS
Menuet dans le style ancien	MARINUZZI
The Mermaids	CATALINI
Valse Caprice	A. RUBINSTEIN
Christmas (December)	TCHAIKOVSKY
Scène dansante	TCHAIKOVSKY
Pas de trois	BENJAMIN GODARD
Panaderos	GLAZOUNOF
Les coquetteries de Colombine	DRIGO
Danse Espagnole	A. RUBINSTEIN
Danse Russe	TCHAIKOVSKY
Menuet	MOZART
Gioconda (Times)	PONCHIELLI